MILLION DOLLAR BOOKS

HAYLEY PAIGE

ONYX PUBLISHING

First published in 2023 by Onyx Publishing, an imprint of Notebook Group Limited, Arden House, Deepdale Business Park, Bakewell, Derbyshire, DE45 1GT.

www.onyxpublishing.com

ISBN: 9781913206833

A CIP catalogue record for this book is available from the British Library.

Typeset by Onyx Publishing of Notebook Group Limited.

Cover art and design by Notebook Group Limited.

ARE YOU READY TO
LAUNCH A BOOK
PUBLISHING COMPANY
AND
WIDEN YOUR NET OF
IMPACT?

For Rob: thank you for your tireless, unwavering, always-uplifting commitment and dedication to me and Onyx Publishing, and the goals you've encouraged me to be brave enough to pursue.

And to my incredible team: you are everything I've imagined building. Every day you allow me to pursue a reality that once was nothing more than a little girl's dreams. I appreciate you all so much.

CONTENTS

PRAISE FOR HAYLEY PAIGE AND ONYX PUBLISHING

Hayley is such a gorgeous person and working with her [presents] such an incredible opportunity. She is amazing.

I achieved a return-on-investment way before my book was even published. And I landed an incredible opportunity for my business as a result of Hayley's blueprinting strategies. It's amazing. Her strategy is pure gold.

I just want everyone to jump in. They'll be so glad they did.

—**JESSA BELLMAN**
Digital Product Coach at jessabellman.com

Hayley Paige really sees people and cares. This is why she is so good at what she does—and I just adore her. I will always be cheering for Hayley!

I feel that I have not only made my dream come true by getting my book into the world, but I have also made wonderful friendships!

—**MARY SWAN-BELL (1973–2022)**
International Bestselling Author of Post-Its and Polaroids

If Hayley's created it, I'm in. I don't even need the details, because if it's with [her], that's all I need to know. Whatever it looks like, count me in. Just send me the link and I'll pay.

—**LORRAINE SCHUCHART**
Founder and CEO at Prosper for Purpose

I'm so glad I joined Hayley's mastermind—I make pages and pages of notes every single call, because she drops gold everywhere she goes. Best decision of 2023! Hayley lays out the process so simply; I've never felt more confident about writing a book. It has helped me level up in so many ways, both personally and in my business, and has already opened up so many opportunities for me. Literally life-changing.

For anyone sitting on the fence... Have the courage and do it.

—LISA A. SMITH
'Retire by 45' Expert & Mentor

I love to go back and listen to [mastermind] replays, even when I've been on the call the first time. I hear new things, and I understand them from a slightly different perspective or with greater depth.

Hayley is a brilliant seeker of information and details that will make a good book into a great book! Her guidance each week keeps my book-writing on track.

A big Thank You to Hayley for being such a great leader, and magically attracting and nurturing us as we evolve into authors.

—WENDY MOORE
Founder and Elite Retreats Host at Elevate & Create

Hayley has created something really special inside her mastermind. It's amazing. It's a whole movement.

When I joined I didn't even know what this was going to become. But it's really beautiful. And I'm just loving the journey.

—ANDEE HOIG
CEO and Publisher at Midlands Business Journal

Hayley deserves all the blessings headed [her] way. Thank you for sharing your gifts and talents. Your impact has a ripple you will never fully see, but I hope that you are able to feel it. I love you big and this is only the beginning!

—**CARRIE RYAN**
Sales and User Experience Mentor

Hayley is a very self-driven, highly motivated individual; her focus and professionalism shines through in all that she does. Furthermore, the team she has chosen to work for her are of the same calibre.

Hayley's high standards have enabled me to showcase my knowledge, experience and know-how. The books [we've published] make me proud whilst also providing me with a solid platform to promote and sell my services and grow my businesses. There's no better business card than a book that makes you an authority in your field!

Hayley, thank you for the opportunity. I am forever grateful for you.

—**EMMA GRANT**
International Bestselling Author of Conscious Parenting

I first met Hayley when she accepted a huge milestone award at an event in California in 2019.

She is an award-winning book publisher who is disrupting the traditional book publishing industry. She continues to inspire me with her words and actions.

—**DONA DEANE**
Leading Marketing and Business Growth Strategist

Hayley's blueprinting process inspired me to create a coaching program based on the book, and I'm also working on a membership as well. I can't thank her enough.

—**GWEN TANNER**
CEO at Planning Awesome

Dreams do come true. Thank you, Hayley Paige, and Onyx Publishing.

—**BRIAN WESTBYE**
International Bestselling Author of Driving Toward Clarity

Hayley's [workshop on How to Successfully Write and Publish Your Book] was one of the best I've ever attended. So valuable.

—**IZZY NALLEY O'DEA**
CEO at Izzy Nalley Consulting

There is only one publisher I would ever recommend, and that's Hayley Paige. She's the go-to accomplished expert. With [Hayley] leading the way, anything is possible!

—**MICHELE HAYES**
Owner at Speaking with Grace

To my editor and publisher Hayley Paige, the queen of dignity and grace, thank you for taking care of my story and your caring heart as we tear away the layers to speak our truth as women. You have become not only my publisher but a dear friend through this process and I will always highly recommend you to any other women who are brave enough to embark on this journey!

—**TRACEY BURGESS**
Wake-Up Down Under

A big thank you to Hayley Paige and her team at Onyx, whose guidance and tough loving care was so central to the outcome.

As I have noted, the process is the product, and working with Hayley and her colleagues has been very special!

—**CHARLES PASCAL (1944–2023)**
Bestselling Author of Leading from the Inside Out

My experience working and learning alongside Hayley and the team has been wonderful. I highly recommend writers give serious consideration to all Hayley and her publishing house have to offer.

—**KAREN GROSE**
International Bestselling Author of The Dime Box

I am so glad you pursued your dream. Your company helped me make one of my dreams come true, too. Thank you for all your hard work and dedication to helping others.

—**KAREN M. ROSNER**
International Bestselling Author of My 12 Hours Aren't Up Yet

Because she is a phoenix, Hayley knows the formula for success. But she doesn't hold the secret of it back; she transfers her knowledge, experience, and even her success to others. She shone, and helps others to shine, too.

She keeps achieving and pushing boundaries, and pushes others to achieve, too. She is simply inspirational.

Now, thanks to Hayley, my book is in Virgin Megastores! If it wasn't for [Hayley], [her] encouragement and all the support [she's] given me, my book [dreams] wouldn't have been realised.

—**SHERIF BENHAWY**
International Bestselling Author of Minds in Battle

Thank you, Hayley. Your [training] was such gold!

—**ASHLEY PÉREZ**
Spiritual Rest Teacher at Enter His Rest

I am so thankful I stumbled across Hayley in a random group one Sunday. She is exactly what I was looking for. Her team is just exceptional and so amazing. I'm already planning my next six books!

—**SCYLLER BORGLUM**
Vice President of WSP USA

Hayley Paige has allowed me, as a female entrepreneur, to reach a level of success and accomplishment that I wouldn't have achieved without becoming a published author. From the very first call to the final publication, every detail was attended to in a manner unsurpassed. Say goodbye to the old ways of becoming an author, and welcome in the new era of publishing with Hayley Paige and Onyx Publishing.

—**SERENA SKINNER**
Certified Magnetic Mind Coach and International Bestselling Author of
The Sex Goddess Diaries

It's so amazing to watch something you poured your heart and soul into come to life.

Thanks, Hayley Paige, for making a huge life dream come true.

—**ASHLEY NAUMANN VONELLA**
CEO at Beauty and the Boss and International Bestselling Author of
How to Be a Corporate Queen

Hayley, Founder of Onyx Publishing, is inspiring in so many ways. Her personality shines with warmth, caring, and reassurance that the publishing process will be pleasant and worth investing time and resources in, with her team supporting me all the way.

I highly recommend working with Hayley and her team.

—**CANDACE MAE**
International Betselling Author of Heaven Within

You're very good at what you do, Hayley, and I appreciate it. So thank you thank you thank you!

—**JEFF HAINBUCH**
International Bestselling Author of The Poet and I

Working with Hayley has been an utter dream. I couldn't be happier that my first publication is with someone like her. Someone who works from the heart. Thank you, Hayley. You and the team have been fantastic and have made the whole process so enjoyable and stress free. I look forward to working together again no doubt in the very near future!

—**ARIANNA TRAPANI**
Founder of The Rapid Growth Academy

The various steps [in the blueprinting process] are *vital*. I've seen holes, and I can see how, if these steps are skipped, the editing process would be compromised.

It's amazing to watch the book become what it wants to be.

—**DARLYNN CHILDRESS**
Parent Coach at Calm Mama Coaching

When you choose Hayley Paige, know your book is in the right hands every step of the way, with every step carefully designed to lead you to success.

Hayley Paige is the best at what she does, and, along your journey, you will find yourself supported and never alone! I just adore her.

—**LORI COOPER**
Industry Insider

The first module of Hayley's Book to Booked workshop had me realizing what I thought I knew about starting to write a book I didn't know! I guess the saying is correct! Thank you, Hayley!

—**CYNTHIA TALLEY**
Financial Freedom Coach for Women

Working with Hayley has been the best experience; the way she takes the book to the next level is really commendable. I think Hayley has created her publishing company as a place to make dreams comes true for thousands of authors.

—**RAGHU NANDANA**
International Bestselling Author of Swadesh

Hayley thrives on the success and encouragement of those of us brave enough to bleed our thoughts and imaginations onto paper. She has allowed her knowledge and skills to guide her publishing house, but it is governed by a far deeper set of core values. Honesty and integrity are at the centre of who Hayley and her business are.

—**T. C. LOWRY**
International Bestselling Author of Arch Recruit

Hayley took me under her wing and was soon raving about my project with as much enthusiasm as I was. I knew Hayley and her publishing house were the only ones who could make [my books] come alive.

Working with Hayley and her team is always a pleasure. If I ever have any questions they're ways answered quickly and the problem is resolved effortlessly. I'm so excited to be working on my second book with them, and can't wait to continue publishing the rest of my series with them too!

—**JORDAN WRIGHT**
International Bestselling Author of The Mandala Chronicles

FOREWORD

When your fellow entrepreneur and close friend specialises in flooding her clients' businesses with hot leads and millions of dollars in untapped revenue, you jump feet-first into her circle and devour every nugget of gold she drops. You listen and learn. You take action like there's no tomorrow. And you turn into a living, breathing billboard, shouting her name to every other professional you know.

The inherent need to share this magic is one reason I am so thrilled this book has been written and sent out into the world.

Meeting Hayley was such a pivotal moment, and completely changed the belief I had in my online business. It was 2020, and I had already achieved financial freedom and retired several years before. I was spending the days enjoying life and its blessings. But I had a nagging inner calling encouraging me to show other women how to gain this extra time and financial freedom. It was while looking for answers and clarity on how to start and grow a business that I came across an online mentoring group and saw one of Hayley's posts.

Very quickly, I came to see that Hayley was one of the most successful entrepreneurs inside the thousands-large group. She was winning awards and being presented with plaques to mark her achievements as she scaled her book publishing company. She was sailing past everyone else, and was very clearly in the upper echelon of the group. What's more, she was posting her progress and details of the steps she had been taking. In other words, she was demonstrating her willingness to share what she had learned and help others along the way.

In everything I do, I look to find the most successful people and model them, and so I went digging for every post I could find to retrace Hayley's steps and learn how she had achieved so much. I was soon fully immersed in Hayley's world—her content, her posts, and the value she so generously shares to empower others to write their books, grow their business, and uplevel in all areas—and there was no going back.

Being realistic, working with Hayley to write and publish your book is a significant investment, and to work 1:1 with her to launch your own publishing company is a greater investment still. But I have had clients who have spent far more on mentoring than Hayley charges, only to receive nothing nearly as valuable as a book (or, indeed, an entire publishing business) in return. My whole philosophy is, if I'm going to make a one-time investment that can achieve a 10X ROI in six to twelve months, it's a complete no-brainer. It just makes sense. And as a professional investor specialising in wealth generation, I would do it as many times as I could, over and over again, because it's just that worth it.

I could not be more sold on what writing and publishing a book can do for your business—and your audience. Hayley once told me that your book is not about you but your readers, and that lesson has stuck with me ever since. To choose not to write your book is to do a disservice to everyone who needs what you have to share—to all the people waiting for your book; to the thousands and thousands it can simultaneously benefit; to those ready and willing to uplevel as a high-ticket client. Imagine the ripple effect of that and how it just keeps on going into forever.

Years have now passed since I first met Hayley in that mentoring circle, and I feel honoured to have watched her journey evolve and progress. I did not ever think we would become such close friends or that there was so much more to her character and work ethic than the initial glimpses social media has to offer. I didn't think, for example, she was the type of person to raise two hundred baby froglets in her reading nook for fear of them being eaten alive by cannibalistic frogs squatting in her garden pond (ask her to share that story with you!), or that she has needed to overcome some very real adversity to create her reality.

What I have come to know and learn about Hayley is that she is incredibly generous, warm, and protective—and she cares about anyone (and anything!) that crosses her path. She is completely overburdened with integrity, and everything she puts out is of an exceptional standard. I've enrolled into her mastermind and been completely blown away, like a kid at a carnival, by what was waiting behind the curtain. I've followed her methods and seen and felt the magic she brings and how she sprinkles that across everything she does. Hayley drops gold every single time I attend a mastermind call or watch one of her trainings—gold that has benefitted me in so many ways inside my business—which is one of the many reasons why I'm so excited this book is now in your hands.

In no time at all, you're going to see what I know to be true: Hayley is not average. You might think you're not a writer. You might have tried to write a book before and given up. You might worry it's going to take too much time. You might even have self-published and seen no results. But none of that matters, because you hadn't met Hayley yet—and the results she will help you achieve are exponential.

You've arrived at the right place. It's time to move through any fear potentially stopping you from enhancing your authority and growing your business.

I understand the fear. I do. I *had* the fear. But just twelve minutes inside Hayley's mastermind changed all of that. One video training was all it took for me to know I was in the right place and my hand was being held every step of the way.

Moving into Hayley's sphere will allow you to widen your reach, influence people who are not currently in your circle, and scale your business with a lead-generating machine that can work for you while you go off and enjoy your life. And the most amazing thing is that a whole world of opportunity and countless doors opening await you.

This right here is the gold standard of assets; a one-time investment for a never-ending return.

The starting point is here, and the time is now.

It's time for the Entrepreneur to achieve Book Success.

—LISA A. SMITH
'Retire by 45' Expert & Mentor

DISCLAIMER

Allow me to pre-frame this entire book by telling you now, in case you don't already know: I am British. This means that you will soon identify the presence of *s* instead of *z* (think *realise* rather than *realize*) and *u* where you might think it doesn't belong (think *colour* and *honour* and *labour*). This is not only intentional but also correct (even if understandably jarring). These aren't mistakes; it's British English. You know, as in English-English.

The same applies to any 'punctuation issues' you might pick up on, such as the additional full stops (*periods*) we sprinkle in to showcase abbreviations, as in the cases of U.K. and U.S.A.

I mention this here so that I'm not bombarded with reviews that mistakenly 'call out' my incorrect spelling and poor punctuation. It's all correct. Full stop. Period.

In this same vein, allow me to reassure you that, when publishing our clients' books, we tend to use American English, predominantly because the majority of our clients are based in the States. But, in mind of my own roots and maintaining the integrity of the language I know and love, my own book adopts British English. (Not to mention, it's obviously the correct version...)

With that said, let's move forward together as we get your book written and published (in whatever version of this language that may be).

Happy writing!

DEAR READERS

WHEN YOUR RESPONSE TO SOMETHING IS TO SAY YOU
DON'T HAVE THE TIME, WHAT YOU'RE ACTUALLY SAYING IS
IT JUST ISN'T A PRIORITY RIGHT NOW.

—GRACE LEVER
Eight-Figure Entrepreneur and Business Mentor

This book has been a long time in the making—not because books should take a long time to write (they shouldn't) and not because I haven't been an expert in my industry for a long, long time (I have), but because there has been an ever-growing wealth of material, strategies, and insider information I have wanted to share with you. I have learned, through this experience of finally taking my book through to publication, that I am flawed and more than able to dish out the advice surrounding 'massive imperfect action' than I am able to take it: I've been stuck in a state somewhere between perfection and hypocrisy, coupled with the absolute knowledge that this time next year and this time in two years (and leading way into forever), there will be new things, new experiences, new lessons, that I want to share with you. But that's all a part of being on these journeys of entrepreneurship and life that see us continuously learning, whether we've been in the industry for seventeen years or not. And, really, let's be honest: there's nothing stopping me, or any of us, from publishing a second edition, should things change or more valuable lessons come to light.

It's so funny to me that more than eighteen months ago, this book was all but done. After blueprinting and outlining every single chapter to the greatest possible degree, I took myself away to a cabin in the woods to focus solely on writing the body of content; four days of uninterrupted bliss. I hadn't, however, factored into the equation that recovering from eye surgery wasn't going to be a walk in the park, and, believing myself to be Supergirl, I arrived at my gorgeous lodge, with its log-burning stove and hot tub, and found that I actually couldn't write, write, write as I'd planned. Instead, in pain and exhausted, I succumbed to the realisation that I needed to heal.

But what was truly miraculous—even for someone as familiar to the process as I am—is the fact I still emerged from that trip with my manuscript halfway to completion. The progress I made was nothing to do with my being a writer and ghostwriter and experienced in my craft; rather, it was everything to do with the blueprint. This detailed roadmap allowed me to make lots of progress (and quick), regardless of the other things I was balancing in my life. This is the very first, most important pillar for any book project.

However, fast-forward to a few weeks before the scheduled Publication Day, and I did the unthinkable: I started my entire book again, from scratch. I found myself reading through material I had written years before and reasoning that there was so much more to give, so many more insights, so much more value. And so, in true Hayley style, I decided to set my goal, restart my project (using the same blueprint as before, of course), and move through the project with the sole objective to give you, my reader, the very best of me.

During this same period of writing, I was also busy with the marketing of the book, practicing what I preach by doing one thing every single day to generate pre-orders and get the word out there.

I was also running my publishing house, leading mastermind calls, engaging on 1:1 calls with Hybrid Ghostwriting clients, overseeing my team, and giving my seal of approval on every single one of our publications, not to mention doing the many things that go with being a mother of three and wife.

During this time, my clients and customers were none the wiser that my book was still in the throes of being written (you are now!), a piece of information I was saving for right here, in this note, for the want to highlight not only the power of a blueprint in allowing you to make massive progress in a very short period of time, but the value of a good publishing house in setting everything up for success while you write and focus on what calls to you in the moment, whether business or family or self-care.

The thing is, this book is important. It's important to me, to what I'm striving to achieve every single day, to my mission to encourage and inspire professionals across the world to write and publish amazing, high-quality lead-generating books, and to be a part of a change in the publishing industry. And I have no doubt it'll prove to be important to the readers who find value in the many different golden nuggets I have intentionally scattered throughout. This isn't my first rodeo, and I've seen many times before (both as an author myself and the CEO of a publishing company leading clients through this very same journey) that the impact can be very real and very profound.

Already, way before it's written and ahead of its publication, my book is touching thousands of people. It has already generated significant revenue for my business. And it is already achieving its goal: to motivate and inspire, and to correct the falsehood and misconception that writing a book needs to be laborious, time consuming, and a general pain in the arse. It doesn't need to be any of those things, and, with the right support, it can actually be the opposite: easy, time efficient, and fun. And it'll also be so worth it, plain and simple.

The book you hold in your hands right now will prove to be something special if you allow it to help you to make progress, and I've been very intentional about facilitating that.

In Part I, you'll find what is essentially the education piece; the *why* underpinning your book and all it can do for you and your business. It'll lead you through quite how powerful a book can be in expanding your reach and widening your net of impact, why now really is the perfect time, and how profitable and lucrative it can be for your bottom line. It'll leave you wondering why you haven't started before now and why it was never a priority, and will encourage you to finally take action.

In Part II, you'll find the *how*, which is focused on helping you to navigate where to start on your book journey, how to give your reader value and position yourself as an authority, what needs to be included (and what you shouldn't include), how to turn your readers into clients, and how you'll know when your first draft is ready to be sent off to your publishing team.

And finally, in Part III, you'll be shown exactly what it takes to achieve book-related success, however it is you personally define it (and, spoiler alert: there is no right or wrong here). I will take you through the different options available to you when you come to publish your book, what you'll need to do to achieve International Bestseller status, and how you can make a book truly work for your business.

This book has been created in mind of getting you started and leading you through the fundamental milestones that will see you making vast progress, without the overwhelm (note the action steps and checklists at the end of some of the chapters; they're there to help you to actually *move*, not sit and look pretty).

Of course, if I were to share every single thing I know—the ins and outs of every task, how to blueprint to the *n*th degree, every single process and hack, and all the different things we do inside our publishing house—this book would go from what some might describe as a standard length to an absolute tome (and, to be frank, all of that is surplus to requirements and way beyond the scope here). As such, this book is geared towards getting you inspired and progressing, and providing the must-have tools and steps needed to see you go from 'Entrepreneur' through to 'Book' and 'Success'.

Of course, there will be a select few readers who feel a little spark of excitement burst into life and intrigue pique with regards the entire publication process and what it can look like behind the scenes. If that is you, whether now or at some stage throughout the book, you might want to consider whether adding an additional arm to your business portfolio in the form of a successful publishing company could present a beautiful alignment for you. If so, you'll find details on how you might start this process, with me and my team as your guide, towards the end of the book.

And for every other reader—the majority of you—who simply want to write and publish a book that will grow your business, you'll find within these pages a whole host of help and direction. You'll also find an additional toolkit in the Resources section of the book, complete with complementary trainings, PDFs, and more, to help you to start *and finish* this project, so that you can emerge with complete clarity as to how to incorporate a book into your business.

Alternatively, if you find that you're completely taken by this book, love the writing, or want to simply cut to the end and outsource this entire project, you also have that option available to you, such as through Hybrid Ghostwriting or Complete Ghostwriting. See Chapter 14 for further details and the Resources section for next steps as, for some, this presents the perfect option and best of all worlds.

Finally, know that I am here for you. I'm a real human being who couldn't be more invested in helping you to succeed. Books and publishing are my life—they make up of so much of what I love, not just my career—and have been very intentionally incorporated into all I have built by design. None of this was an accident; rather, it is the culmination of the dreams and aspirations of a six-year-old little girl manifested:

I dreamt of launching a publishing house. I made this happen.

I scaled that publishing house with clear-cut goals centred on helping people to write and publish good books.

I created a Bestseller program.

I crafted a book-planning and -blueprinting program.

I built a suite of different programs and offers that are aligned and resonate with my Dreamy Client base.

And now, fast-forward more than ten years, to 2023, I find myself the owner of an award-winning boutique book publishing company with thirteen different products and services, and a completely exclusive opportunity to teach other entrepreneurs how to do the same.

It is with this said—with you safe in the knowledge that this is far more than a business, but actually one of my true loves—that I invite you to reach out and let me know where you're at in this journey; when you reach key milestones, when you have breakthroughs, and when you emerge from a chapter or section with a takeaway that's changed something for you. I'd love to know. Honestly, it will mean the world.

You can contact me on hayley@entrepreneurbooksuccess.com.

Sending you all my best wishes as you begin (and also handing you a bucket for all the gold you'll soon be scooping up as you move through each page). Thank you for choosing me to guide you.

INTRODUCTION

'**Y**ou *don't have the time* to add six or seven figures to your revenue right now?'

The Atlantic Ocean and four thousand miles separate me from Emily, and I await her response. She looks up and off to the side as I pose the ultimate question, leaving her to truly contemplate.

I knew when I asked the question—just like I know every single time I put this same train of thought to a fellow entrepreneur or business owner who has long been debating writing their book, only to arrive at the conclusion that 'they don't have the time right now'—that it wouldn't land comfortably. I knew, before the words had even left my lips, that Emily would start to consider giving me her well-rehearsed excuse.

I know now, after so many conversations like this one, that on the very tip of her tongue, a rationalisation is forming as to why, despite apparently having wanted it so badly and for so long, time continues to steal right from under her any sense of autonomy she might have, completely destroying her book-writing plans in the process.

But I'm not here to ask the easy questions and fill both my and Emily's precious time with fluff. Emily has reached out to *me*, booked in a call with *me*, sought expertise and needle-moving steps from *me*, so the least I can do is honour our time together by making sure she leaves the conversation with complete clarity and the recognition that if she wants this, she can really, truly make it happen—and far easier and quicker than she might think.

In the same vein, I also really want her to understand that if she chooses not to move forward, that's exactly it: she is *choosing* not to move forward.

'Ahh, I know, I know,' she says. 'I've wanted to do this for years. Decades, actually. Obviously I have, or I wouldn't have asked to speak with you.'

It's a small breakthrough.

'So,' I broach, 'considering we all have the same twenty-four hours in a day, and bearing in mind we each have the freedom to choose at least where some of that time goes—career, home life, kids, basic needs of sleeping and eating, etcetera, aside—and even throwing into the mix that you could make progress on your book journey with just two hours a week—which we can all spare, let's be honest; it's seventeen minutes a day—it's safe to say time isn't the real issue. So what do you think actually *is* holding you back from taking the right steps and making this happen?'

She takes a big breath and sighs. 'I think we both know the answer to that. I'm scared to death.'

This book is about what you need to do to incorporate a book into your business as a critical component in your marketing strategy.

It's about how needle-moving and freeing that step can be, and why some of the most successful and globally recognised entrepreneurs, coaches, mentors, thought leaders, speakers, experts, and professional service providers have chosen to harness the power of a book in their business—not just once, but many times over.

But as well as the 'how-to' and the huge results, it's also about the roadblocks people project onto their own path to obstruct and self-sabotage their progress, whether consciously or subconsciously, and quite how hindering that can be in the pursuit of business growth and the streamlining of sales.

As the founder and CEO of an award-winning boutique book publishing company specialising in lead-generating books, it's deeply frustrating to me when an otherwise-driven, high-achieving expert says they are committed to writing and publishing a book—a book with massive potential to grow their business—only to then watch as they delay (or even indefinitely put on hold) the start of their book journey.

It may sound dramatic, but my heart breaks a little every time, because I know the reason for that delay is usually fear.

It could be fear surrounding how the book will be received; bad reviews, maybe.

It might be fear stemming from the actual content and story being shared; the truth upsetting people in the author's close circle.

It could be fear that the book won't sell; the message failing to resonate.

It might be that impostor syndrome has taken up residence in their head: *You're not qualified to write a book. Who do you think you are?*

And, as strange as it might sound, it might even be the fear of a greater degrees of success. New level, new devil, so to speak.

By the end of this book, however, it is my hope—well, more than that; it is my *ultimate goal*—for you to have complete clarity on the immense power you can harness with a book, both personally and professionally, and to get you to a place of real excitement and inspiration, not only in recognition of its sheer potential, but also in regards the simplicity, ease, and speed with which one can come together.

It is my hope that, even before you've closed this book, you'll find yourself thick in the throes of blueprinting, writing, or publishing. It may be that you'll reach out to join our self-guided book-writing program or our group mastermind. Maybe you'll want to discuss ghostwriting or start the publication process for a first draft completed long ago. You might even take things a step further and decide books are too powerful in business and the entrepreneurial bubble as a whole for you not to consider launching your very own publishing house. Whatever your journey, I am determined to help you progress it in the most professional, authority-boosting way.

This isn't to say you won't experience moments of doubt; that you won't question whether you're qualified to write and even whether your business is in the right place for a book. But it *is* to say that you'll see, clear as day, your fear is worth overcoming. The benefits are simply too great and too numerous not to be reaped. Because really, if I were to shine a spotlight on the fact that you could activate a stream of warm, self-qualifying leads into your business, add six or seven figures to your annual revenue (multiple seven figures if adding a publishing house to your own business portfolio), boost your authority and status in your niche, and have leads pay to become leads, all simply by writing and publishing a book, wouldn't you reason that any fear you have—impostor syndrome, triggering friends and family, whether or not you're truly qualified to write a book—would fall away into a void of insignificance?

It's all about cost–benefit, and the potential wins far outweigh any hypothetical, might-not-even-happen fears and the delay tactics that conveniently go along with them.

One of my mentors, Lisa Smith, who specialises in helping women to become financially free and retire by forty-five years old, told me once: the first voice is always your true voice; the second voice that follows—the one that tells you why you can't do something or how you might fail—is the fear voice; the voice keeping you stuck in a place of perceived safety and comfort, so that you don't feel tempted to explore the 'dangers' of the unknown. The first voice is the voice to be listened to. I share this with you because that lesson has stuck with me, and it helps me to navigate fear and separate what I truly want from what fear tells me is (or, more accurately, is *not*) possible.

Armed with the information I will share in this book, you will emerge from its final pages knowing the value of this incredible marketing platform. You will truly understand the role a book can play in both the professional and personal facets of your life, as demonstrated through many different lenses. You will be clear on the figures surrounding book-writing and -publication in relation to the cost of leads and other efficiency-based in-business factors. And, most importantly, you will know exactly how to get started with your lead-generating book so that you can make productive, needle-moving progress. This will be the case for you regardless of where you currently stand on your path to Entrepreneur, Book, Success: whether you are at the stage of merely nurturing a seedling of an idea and are looking for that gentle nudge from the universe and handholding to get started; whether you need details on exactly what components you should be including and how to navigate the blueprinting and writing journey in a business-boosting way; whether you've completed a first draft and need the roadmap on what steps to take next to ensure you have maximised on the potential of a lead-generating non-fiction book (i.e. you haven't missed out critical elements and can progress on to achieve professional, well-respected standards of publication).

You will also be gifted with a wealth of high-value resources to assist you on this amazing journey, not only as a thank-you for buying and reading this book, but as a helping hand with actually getting started and making progress.

WHY ENTREPRENEUR. BOOK. SUCCESS.™?

Throughout my career as the builder and nurturer of my publishing house (as I write, our business is ten years old), I have had the pleasure of working with an incredible number of high-achieving, driven, success-focused business owners, and it has been a truly beautiful experience providing a wealth of insight. It has allowed me to dig deep into my tribe's motivations for writing a book, as well as the factors that keep them stuck in a state of progress paralysis. It has allowed me to identify their most common pain points and where they ultimately want to be. The end goals are always super-clear: they want to write a well-received book that positions them as an authority; they want to achieve International Bestseller status; and they want to have a high-value, larger-than-life lead magnet they can hand out to qualified prospects to nurture into their business.

Of course, those end goals are rarely ever framed in this way. Instead, my clients will tell me that they want to write a book and that they know it can work for their business but they're not sure how to get there, before then usually going on to subtly ask, 'And what about Bestseller status? Can you achieve that?'

The problem, however, is that despite them knowing what they want, they simply don't know how to get there. They don't know where to start, how long it's going to take, and whether it will be as painful, torturous, and time consuming as the narrative around book-writing seems to be. (By the way, I promise you it really isn't anything like that—and if a past experience tells you it is, quite honestly, you were approaching it all wrong.) And so they give up. They give up because they're looking for a reason to give up—to talk themselves out of it—because of so many of the aforementioned fear-rooted thoughts swirling around their minds.

This then leads to what could have been someone's next favourite book simply not being written. (Again, ever so slightly heartbreaking.)

At this point, when these narratives start echoing in our minds and when we speak to ourselves in the most degrading ways about why we're so far from qualified to write a book, I would urge you to ask yourself the following:

Did you know how to launch a business when you first started out?

Did you know how to scale it?

Did you know how to craft offers and opportunities for your Dream Clients?

Did you know how to invite people into those opportunities?

Did you know the ins and outs of contracts, payment processers, refund policies, and even the legalities surrounding business?

Or did you think to yourself, *I want to start my own business*, and then take the leap of faith, confident in the fact that you were intelligent and driven enough to figure everything else out along the way?

Writing a book is no different. Well, actually, it really is, in that it's infinitely easier. Plus, you have here in your hands a highly valuable go-to resource to help you along the way.

If you can launch and scale a successful business, you can certainly write a book. (And, for the record, objectively speaking, you qualify as having a 'successful business' if you're generating revenue, whether it's five figures or eight, especially if, once upon a time, that business didn't even exist.)

Importantly, however, it's critical you have the mindset piece in place when starting your writing and publishing journey. For one, it's so easy to throw in the towel partway through, or even right at the very end. I've known people to write an entire manuscript and then do nothing with it for years; abandoning the task after all the hard work is already done.

It's also important to be realistic and know that nothing is ever a complete walk in the park: those moments of doubt will come, negative reviews will come, and quiet sales months will come, but it's all a process. This very sentiment was echoed by one of my amazing clients, the late Charles Pascal (an internationally recognised educator and author with expertise in early and higher education, public policy, leadership, and strategic philanthropy), who said to me as we went to publication with his book, 'The process is the product.'

It's a journey, and one that's meant to be enjoyed; one you embark on in your own time, whether with slow, measured steps or in a quicker, hungry-for-the-benefits way.

However you approach the process, writing a book can be incredibly liberating—both professionally and personally—and will give you an amazing sense of achievement—and that's without all of the other tangible and intangible benefits that will come your way. This is something my clients know and recognise.

They know they need to write their book.

They know now is absolutely the right time.

They trust themselves to locate the right resources and implement, even if they don't initially know where to start.

And they jump at the golden opportunity to begin when those resources become available.

And truly, that's all anyone else who's completed this process before them has done; found the right tools and processes and moved forward with motivation and a deep inner knowing that their book needs to be out there.

The important thing is to start—to start *now*—even if that starting point is merely reading this book and nurturing the idea of elevating your platform with a book. It's all progress.

Entrepreneur. Book. Success.™ will help you to widen your reach and have your message create a ripple effect across the globe. It will help you, whether as a startup entrepreneur or well-established seven- or eight-figure business owner, to go from feeling unsure in what is a completely unfamiliar process, to walking a very solid, well-laid path, knowing what time needs to be assigned to the task, where to start, where to go next, where to finish, how to *know* when you're finished, and how to publish to a standard that is reflective of the standards you incorporate in your day-to-day practices, programs, and services.

For some readers, it will highlight the desire to outsource the entire process, such as through a completely Done-For-You Ghostwriting and Publication approach, whereas others might opt for a middle ground of

Hybrid Ghostwriting™.

Whatever calls to you can work, and all routes can lead you across the finish line with a book in-hand you will be proud of for months, years and decades to come.

But remember that adopting a laser focus for productivity is *not* synonymous with perfectionism:

The pursuit of perfection is relentless and unforgiving, halting progress and keeping you rooted. It's like a beast that, if permitted to gatecrash your life even once, will go on to critique every move that follows. More relevantly, you'll never meet the high standards required by perfection: they're ever-moving and evasive, and they change like the wind depending on how your inner perfectionist feels that day. So, I would always advise: as much as your book should be beautifully aligned with all you do in your business and the standards you adhere to and maintain in everything you do, prioritise making progress and crafting what your clients need in this moment. In other words, write a book that serves them. The frills really aren't that important. Instead, leave your publisher to do all the finetuning, polishing, and refining. You'll find the reception of a written book infinitely warmer than the reception of an abandoned, part-written manuscript (i.e. none whatsoever!), and you might even find that your high-value creative output creates the foundation of a powerful legacy.

My advice? Abandon perfection, pursue progress, and invest in building a legacy.

You've got this (if you want it).

TO BE FEARLESS AND DETERMINED

As I've mentioned previously, while this book doesn't seek to explore in depth the mindset piece that is critical to every entrepreneurial undertaking (including that of writing and publishing a book), it nonetheless is essential that as you progress through every stage, you remind yourself of the following:

Your business deserves to be even more successful.

Those who need you are relying on you to find and reach them.

You have huge amounts of value to share.

You don't need to be a writer; you just need to be an expert.

Book success can absolutely be yours.

A book allows your business name and brand to touch new audiences.

Your book can allow you to reach prospects moving in unexplored spaces in your orbit.

A book allows you to instantly uplevel your authority in your niche.

Everyone who is meant to be in your container will love what you share.

With all of this said, it's obvious: your book needs to be written.

I am honestly so excited to begin this journey with you!

ACTION STEPS: INTRODUCTION

1. Send me an email on hayley@entrepreneurbooksuccess.com. Title it, *I'm reading EBS!* and tell me:
    o   Why is now the perfect time for you to write and publish a book?
    o   What is your ultimate goal for this book?
    I promise to read your email (and I will always respond to as many as I possibly can).
2. Take a photograph of you holding the book and post it to social media, declaring your commitment to leveraging a book in your business. Use the hashtag #EntrepreneurBookSuccess. I'll share it to my platforms.
3. Join our Facebook group, which is exclusively available to readers of this book, and share your thoughts and breakthroughs on this introductory chapter:
    www.facebook.com/groups/entrepreneurbooksuccess.
4. Complete the Book Goals Worksheet:
    www.entrepreneurbooksuccess.com/bookgoals.
    By allowing yourself to get clear on exactly what results and benefits (both tangible and intangible) you can achieve by writing a book and incorporating it as a part of your business marketing strategy, you'll come to truly resonate with the value to be reaped and fully understand the true importance of making progress and

seeing this project through to the end.
5. And, finally, if you feel like the fear piece is rearing its ugly head and you're listening to the second voice more than the first voice, I've put together a short video training on mindset. Go and take a look: www.entrepreneurbooksuccess.com/mindset.

CHECKLIST: INTRODUCTION

1. Sent me an email.
2. Took a photograph and posted to various social media platforms using #EntrepreneurBookSuccess.
3. Joined our Facebook group and shared your thoughts and breakthroughs.
4. Completed the Book Goals Worksheet.
5. Watched the Mindset video training.

PART I: ENTREPRENEUR

CHAPTER 1
A LEAD-GENERATING BOOK

I AM EXPERIENCED ENOUGH TO DO THIS. I AM
KNOWLEDGEABLE ENOUGH TO DO THIS. I AM PREPARED
ENOUGH TO DO THIS.

—ALEXANDRIA OCASIO-CORTEZ
U.S. Representative

A BOOK IS A COMPLETE NO-BRAINER

A BOOK IS ONE OF the most valuable, lucrative, and well-performing platforms any entrepreneur can utilise in their business. Whether you're looking to grow your business by attracting in more primed-to-buy leads as you pursue consistency or you'd love to throw rocket fuel on your already-thriving business, a book is a strategic piece I would encourage you to urgently begin incorporating into your marketing.

The real beauty of a lead-generating authority-stamping book (such as the one I will walk you through planning and writing here) is that it can work for any entrepreneur, business owner, thought leader, or professional services provider, regardless of the niche in which you operate. All you really need is the experience and results that come from walking your clients through a high-value transformation.

It could be that you help your clients to progress from the 'feast or famine' stress of sporadic $10K months, to operating from a place of abundance at consistent $50K months.

It could be that you support your clients in navigating trauma, healing, and achieving peace in their day-to-day lives.

Maybe it's leveraging PR to uplevel and open doors to opportunity and entrepreneurial success.

It could even be navigating divorce or coparenting, or planning a wedding on a budget.

The niche and subject aren't necessarily what really matter, and they certainly don't qualify or disqualify a business owner from writing and publishing a book. The important thing is that you have a business with a validated offer, and that you are able to help your Ideal Clients to move from 'problem' to 'solution'.

With these components in place, a lead-generating book is a complete no-brainer for you and your business. With just a little time and effort as you move through the book-planning, -writing, and -publication processes (or *very* little time and effort, if you opt for a Done-For-You approach, such as ghostwriting), you'll soon find yourself with a professionally crafted book that works for you and your business, regardless of how present you are.

Do it once, and it will continue to work for you forever. I have watched this happen again and again for my clients.

Every single month, I sit down with my team and go over the monthly royalties reports sent out to our clients. In these moments, from within the walls of our publishing house, I can see how well our lead-generating books continue to sell and sell year after year after year, consistently and organically, even when their authors take their foot off the marketing pedal.

This works so well because of the formulae we follow in our business, not only when it comes to helping our clients to blueprint and outline their books (with key emphasis on the transformational journey you need to take your reader on), but with every single stage of the publication process: the cover design, title and subtitle creation, and blurb-writing, amongst others.

It's all so very simple and straightforward. It can and will work for you and your business, and it will work far better than any other strategy, whether conversational marketing (relentlessly time consuming), paid ads (regular cash injections required), or live trainings, webinars, and workshops (energetically sapping). All you truly need is the want to leverage a book in your business, the belief in the results you help your clients to achieve, and a willingness to take action.

The only way this *won't* work for you is if you don't see it through, if you delay or procrastinate or make excuses, if you allow fear to keep you stuck, or if you feel like this just isn't a priority right now. And quite honestly, if any of the above show even a glimmer of possibility, I would highly recommend you save yourself a lot of time and just put this book down now.

If, on the other hand, you are the type to leap at golden opportunities and apply yourself with an energy and passion that you know seriously allows you to quantum leap time and time again, this book is for you. Whether your action taking takes the form of you outsourcing this entire project to someone else or sitting down to do the work yourself, this book will provide you with the next steps in this journey.

And I'm so excited for that journey.

A BOOK THAT GENERATES LEADS

Before you fully commit to this journey and start moving through to the *how* stages, I first want to be super-clear here as to exactly what a lead-generating book is.

I remember a short while ago one of my business acquaintances told me that, although she'd seen me use the phrase 'lead-generating book' for years and years, she had never known exactly what it meant. Although that kind of blew my mind—I had thought it was pretty self-explanatory—I want to be absolutely sure that we move forward with clarity, with none of the critical, foundational pieces either missing or confusing.

With this said, a lead-generating book is, simply put, a book that generates leads. That's the bottom line; what it says on the tin is what's inside the tin. It's a book that works for you, as a part of your overall marketing and sales strategy, with the overarching purpose of attracting readers, turning them into leads, and directing them to your business, with the ultimate goal of converting as many of those leads into clients as possible.

Of course, all of this is done in the most professional, customer-centric way, and that's through providing value, solving as many pain points as you possibly can (without giving away the ingredients to your high-level programs), and helping your reader to make real progress towards their dream results.

Throughout this book, we'll discuss exactly how this is done.

A BETTER WAY OF DOING BUSINESS

When I first established our publishing house in July 2013, the entrepreneurial boom was really beginning to find its feet. Very quickly, I found myself immersed in a world that was full to bursting with the most amazing potential: men and women across the globe were learning to monetise their passions and skills, follow their soul's purpose, and launch businesses focused on providing high-level products and services. Overnight, hope was flooding into the lives of regular, everyday people, taking them from low-earning jobs and high-stress corporate roles to five- and six-figure days spent providing soul-centred services to the dreamiest of clients.

It was and is amazing, and it continues to blow my mind.

However, I'm sure I'm not the only business owner to have questioned, at various points in my journey, whether I have actually created a monster.

Without much warning, in 2019, I made a commitment to myself that I would direct every bit of my energy to scaling my publishing house. I handed my successful editing business over to my eldest daughter, and despite having three children (one of whom was a ten-month-old baby), I threw myself into my goal and did everything I could to achieve the ultimate balancing act of all balancing acts: scaling to a million-dollar business.

Over the course of nothing more than a few short weeks, I had enrolled into business mentoring and set about implementing every strategy I came across to pave the way to success. Fast implementation quickly became my jam, and before I knew it, it was one of the things I had become known for in and across my newfound entrepreneurial circles. Suddenly, I went from being completely anonymous to feeling anything but, and new clients and projects were coming out of my ears. It was amazing, of course—I had created an incredible business that was clearly in demand, presenting the world with a completely new hybrid model and way of writing and publishing—but the stress and overwhelm were both very real. I had to quickly step up and take to heart the absolute essence of being a business owner, and that meant learning a million and one different things I had never heard of: conversational marketing, lead magnets, email nurtures, discovery calls, webinars, live workshops, funnels, CRMs... the list goes on. And this was all while I was learning how to really put myself out there for the first time.

The most difficult of those times centred on the sales calls and lack of anonymity. As a complete introvert and camera-shy individual (never mind someone who had at that point been very intentionally building a private life away from social media), I found the mere concept of discovery calls and social media livestreams extremely stressful and anxiety-inducing. Invite strangers to book in face-to-face calls and sell my services? No, thank you! Go live on Facebook and run a sixty-minute workshop on professional publication? Nope! I was neither an extrovert nor a sales professional. The thought was terrifying. Nevertheless, I knew I had to push through the fear if the business was to be successful. And so, like anything we commit to learning and excelling at, I soon got used to (and became very proficient at) discovery calls, interacting on livestreams, hopping onto impromptu Zoom calls, and running workshops and events.

As a result, the company was growing, and my name was being thrown around the entrepreneurial sphere, complete with my 'booking in' link. I soon had a consistently fully booked call schedule, and my days were exhaustingly long.

Although this was amazing, there were key problems:

Those booking in calls weren't qualified.

They weren't sold on why they should write and publish a book.

They weren't ready to take the action steps.

They weren't ready to take their business to the next level.

Rather, they had quite simply wanted to reach out and gather the information for 'one day'.

And, in some cases, they had booked a call to 'make a friend with a fellow entrepreneur'.

None of that was their fault, of course, but mine: I'd left myself and our business wide open to that possibility. But that didn't mean it needed to stay that way.

I knew we needed warm, ready-to-move leads.

People who were genuinely feeling the pull and the nudge to write their book and get it out there.

Leads who were self-qualifying, who knew who they needed to be in order to work with us.

Leads that were ready to take action now—not 'one day', not at a 'better time', but now.

Leads who were at the right stage in their business.

Leads with questions, yes, but not debilitating objections.

Leads who could jump into our book-planning, publication, ghostwriting, or other programs with nothing more than a few questions posed via email or DM.

This clarity as to what we needed—and *wanted*—was when I truly started to dig deep and stop winging things:

I thought back to the first non-fiction book I'd ever written, way before I even knew about authority and lead-generating books and how they could work for a business. Back then, in 2015, when I was only two years into my publishing business but eight years into my career in the industry, I'd accidentally but very successfully written a book that created huge value for its readers and—again accidentally—directed them into my editing business (note: not my publishing house). That book, which gave away all the gold I had at that time, still succeeded in achieving incredible results:

New clients into my business.

Superfans who followed my every (online) move.

And countless messages every single day thanking me for writing the book.

That very short read grew my audience with new followers, new prospects, new clients, and an audience that still reaches out to me to this very day.

Non-fiction books focused on business, I realised, had the potential to be complete game-changers.

I remember feeling a wave of simultaneous excitement and relief wash over me as I sat in my home office, walking my then-boyfriend (now husband) through my experience, and the rest, as they say, is history.

Since then, I have led countless clients through the process of planning, writing, and publishing business-growing books. I have ghostwritten many. And I have loved being witness to the transformations these books have had. It's honestly truly remarkable.

Since that epiphany, we've focused on books that are written with the specific objective of increasing revenue for the author's business and elevating the authority and status of the business owner to derive many amazing benefits. One of the biggest advantages is it can completely transform how your business is run, especially if you are still in a place of generating leads with organic methods, such as conversational marketing and discovery calls. A book has the power to warm and nurture leads (and not just any leads, but leads that pay to become leads), with those leads then self-qualifying for your services. This means that, by the time your prospects/readers decide that working with you is the right next step in their journey, they will already be in possession of all the critical information: what you help your clients to achieve; what working with you looks like; what results they can expect; what you expect of your clients; who they need to be in order to work with you; the investment required; how they go about taking the next step.

Consider for a moment if all your leads—whether cold, warm, or hot—knew all of this before even reaching out to you or your team. Would they need to book in discovery calls? A large percentage of them wouldn't, because they would already have the information they need. Now think about how that would not only impact the efficiency of your business, but how much leaner and more streamlined your sales and onboarding processes could be.

A lead-generating non-fiction book is a goldmine of potential, and the financial benefits concern not only the revenue generated, but the overheads saved.

I say it on a daily basis, whether to my team, on podcasts, or during live events and interviews, but a book is a complete no-brainer, and it's unlike any other marketing platform out there. I know—I did it accidentally for my own business way before I even started helping my clients to do it. It allows you to achieve benefits and success business-wide—and that's truly incredible.

ENTREPRENEUR + BOOK = SUCCESS

I have the strongest and most unwavering belief in the power of a book in business—and I know because I've seen, time and time again, that when you have a high-achieving, coachable entrepreneur with a determined mindset who is ready to incorporate a book as a needle-moving marketing element in their business, they can achieve even greater levels of success.

The most important factor, however, is ensuring the presence of all the important pieces. If those are there, we can very quickly apply the following equation:

$$\text{Entrepreneur} + \text{Book} = \text{Success}$$

We can even go so far as to state that, with the inclusion of all the necessary components, we'll also find the following to be true:

$$\text{Entrepreneur Book} = \text{Success}$$

And moreover, when considering the network, contacts, email lists, and overall reach of entrepreneurs and business owners, coupled with their (whether learned or natural) ability to sell, every entrepreneur can position themselves to achieve book success. This is otherwise translated to:

$$\text{Entrepreneur} = \text{Book Success}$$

Importantly, however (and I will reiterate this again and again throughout this book), it's super-important to incorporate all the must-haves to achieving success in the specific lead-generating non-fiction book arena—and not only that, but to progress through several different stages. These include:

- Being sold on the idea of a book.
- Being clear about (and strategically determining) exactly what concept or idea you want to explore in your book.
- Understanding the journey your prospects/readers will be taken on, and exactly what that needs to look like.
- Getting clear on exactly what to include—and what not to include.
- Understanding how to attract your Ideal Client/reader by crafting a title and subtitle in line with our recommended formula.
- Going to pre-order and starting to generate interest and orders before even writing a single word of your book.
- Positioning yourself as the expert.
- Learning how to apply one of a number of different writing techniques to get your book written quickly (or otherwise choosing to hire a ghostwriter).
- Understanding how to incorporate lead-generation into your book, both subtle and direct.
- Crafting an exclusive lead magnet (or several) for your readers in mind of providing value and elevating your expertise.
- Researching and including a wealth of resources and links in your book.
- Determining the most effective and efficient route to publication.
- Initiating your ongoing marketing campaign.
- Making your book truly work for your business.

And all whilst recognising the super-important point that you don't need to be a writer: you just need to be able to help your clients achieve results. Say it out loud:

I don't need to be a writer. I just need to be able to help my clients achieve results.

This book, which is broken down into three parts (namely 'Entrepreneur', 'Book', and 'Success'), will take you by the hand and guide you across all stages of relevance. As the culmination of seventeen years of industry experience, it offers insight and a wealth of value to help you to either begin or continue your book journey and subsequently uplevel your business.

I don't need to be a writer. I just need to be able to help my clients achieve results.

The structure of this book has been carefully considered in mind of it allowing you to either read from one chapter to the next or to dance around from one section or chapter to another, depending on where you are at in the process. You do not need to read in sequential order to reap value or incorporate key teachings; rather, feel free to throw yourself into whatever part of the process is inspiring to you at any given moment.

I don't need to be a writer. I just need to be able to help my clients achieve results.

And, of course, please, please, please make use of the resources made available to you throughout the book (which are also available all in one place in the Resources section at the back of this book), as every single additional PDF, video training, template, or program can help you to achieve even more—and then more and more again.

My work in and exploration of every single area of writing and publishing—fuelled by my hunger and passion for the publishing industry as a whole—throughout the past seventeen years means that, if you commit to reading this book, utilising the resources, and taking your book as seriously as you would take any other project in your business (whether ads, funnels, or workshops), you can expect to emerge from the experience with a huge amount of clarity regarding what your next steps should be and how success can be yours. Plus, your enthusiasm will burn so hot and bright that you'll be kicking yourself for not boarding this train all the way to Destination Publication earlier in your career!

I don't need to be a writer. I just need to be able to help my clients achieve results.

The journey I have been on since launching our publishing house has, both professionally and personally, been so incredibly transformational, not only for me as a CEO and leader, but as the owner of a boutique book publishing company that is laser-focused on helping entrepreneurs to harness the power of a book in their business. I am determined to build a community of high-achieving entrepreneurs who believe in and live out the Entrepreneur. Book. Success.™ journey, and I would love for you to join me—but only if you're ready to move through any fear and objections and do this now.

ACTION STEPS: CHAPTER 1

1. Get clear: Detail the key benefits you can see for why you would write a lead-generating book to grow your business. This will keep you pushing forward.
2. Remind yourself aloud: *I don't need to be a writer. I just need to be able to help my clients achieve results.* If you aren't confident in your writing skills, note this down—like an affirmation—and remind yourself of this every single day.
3. Share your key takeaways for Chapter 1 inside the Facebook group: www.facebook.com/groups/entrepreneurbooksuccess

CHECKLIST: CHAPTER 1

1. Established exactly why I should write a book to elevate my business.
2. Committed to reminding myself that I don't need to be a writer to do this well.
3. Shared my key takeaways for Chapter 1 inside the Facebook group.

CHAPTER 2
THE BENEFITS OF A BOOK IN YOUR BUSINESS

NO MATTER WHAT PEOPLE TELL YOU, WORDS AND
IDEAS CAN CHANGE THE WORLD.

—ROBIN WILLIAMS (1951–2014)
Actor; quoted from Dead Poets Society

WHAT WE KNOW ABOUT EXPERTS WITH BOOKS

IT'S NEITHER DEEP NOR COMPLEX: quite simply, we know books can elevate businesses, enhance the authority of the author/business owner, increase revenue, and reduce overheads—and all without talent, skills, or investments that are particularly extreme or out of the ordinary.

Of course, that isn't to say that those writing lead-generating non-fiction books don't possess exceptional skills in their arena—they absolutely do—but it is to say that you don't need to uplevel your writing skills or be able to craft eloquent, descriptive prose to achieve the goal of writing and publishing a book.

When we consider how books expand the reach of the author and ultimately introduce readers to the various products and services the author offers, it's easy to see why entrepreneurial experts across the world write books—and you have to ask yourself: if so many high-level entrepreneurs pursue this venture, doesn't that suggest there's value to be found here?

I assure you: these books aren't being written in the pursuit of earning a little extra in publisher-paid royalties (far from it, considering traditional publishers retain as much as 95% of all royalties). It's because books achieve growth.

Think Richard Branson. Stormy Wellington. Danielle Newman. Steve Jobs. Tony Robbins. Angela Duckworth. Tiffany Haddish. Carrie Green. It's all about brand exposure, company growth, additional revenue, respect, authority—but, most importantly, lead-generation; after all, that's the lifeblood of any business.

What's more, it's not only about introducing readers to the ways you can help your prospects; rather, books present an incredible opportunity for you to simply introduce yourself to the world—or even reintroduce yourself!—because books have amazing potential when it comes to creating a community of superfans.

Superfans are the people who know, like, and trust you, come to love you, and appreciate and align with all you stand for, all you represent, how you carry yourself, how you nurture your business and your clients, and how you show up in the world. Imagine how many Facebook™ ads, emails, lives, and different touchpoints you would need to make that same connection.

Books are a marketing platform, and that includes allowing not only your business and services to be marketed on a global scale, but you and your name.

THE BENEFITS: AN OVERVIEW

The benefits of writing and publishing a lead-generating book that will work for you and your business (even when you're not working) never fail to blow my mind. They are not only numerous, but also far greater than the benefits reaped from other lead-generating/client attraction methods. I say this not as the CEO of a publishing house (who you could understandably consider to be biased), but as a fellow entrepreneur and business owner. As a professional looking to simultaneously grow my business and work only with the dreamiest of clients, a book offers the very best of all client acquisition strategies.

The results are incredible, and therefore deserve a spotlight of their own.

YOUR LEADS PAY TO BECOME LEADS

This is perhaps one of the most amazing benefits a lead-generating book can offer its business owner author, and it continues to amaze me.

Every time someone buys a copy of your book, you will earn a royalty. This royalty might be $5, or it might be $20. This ultimately depends on several different factors, such as the print costs of your book, the sale price, and the percentage of royalties your publisher takes (note: we don't take any percentage of our authors' royalties). Whatever that figure, you will be receiving money and be 'in the green', so to speak.

By purchasing your book, your prospect is taking a step to solve their problem and paying you to help them. When taking the step to buy your book (which is essentially a low-ticket offer), your lead (the reader) is asking you to guide them in moving forward and is clearly communicating to you (the author and expert) not only their need for assistance, but their readiness to embark on that journey. If your book has been written and published in the right way, the reader will then enter your orbit and position themselves as a lead, enabling you to capture their details and nurture them moving forward. If done the wrong way, however, your reader will stay just that: a reader.

Compare this situation with, for example, paid ads. Of course, ads have their place and can be extremely powerful in growing and scaling and acquiring new leads for your business. However, ads require many more touchpoints, consistent cash injections, as well as knowledge and expertise, if you are to strike the right balance between the costs to acquire a new lead and the revenue generated for the business. Moreover, a certain number of leads need to be brought into the business 'funnel' before one pays for a product or service and makes the ads profitable (or allows the business to break even).

In the case of a book, on the other hand (if done correctly), every reader will become a lead and every lead will mean immediate profit for you (the author). This means that every single time someone purchases a copy and enters your professional world, your business is making money while growing its audience of potential clients—not the case for paid ads, with many business owners happy simply to break even. This also means that any subsequent low-, medium-, or high-ticket services absolutely crush typical ROI on ad spend.

Of course, this isn't to say that ads can't be profitable. I fully believe they can be. However, I also fully believe it takes a lot of potentially very expensive trial-and-effort, not to mention multiple touch points, before finding an ad that means investing $1 and achieving a ROI on a per-lead basis.

Using a book as a lead-acquisition system, on the other hand, means there is no need to worry if one thousand new leads have clicked onto your ad and opted into a free offer but not bought an upsell, thereby putting your advertising budget 'in the red'. This means no longer considering when to deactivate your ads and, as a result, putting a halt to your influx of new leads because your business is haemorrhaging money through ad spend. Instead, you'll receive new prospects into your business every single time a copy of your book is sold (or even given away to your Ideal Client), and you can let your book do the work in warming your reader, nurturing the relationship, and directing them to your business.

READERS ARE DREAMY PROSPECTS

As a demographic, readers have characteristics that make them desirable as clients, regardless of the niche or industry in which your business operates (and for the sake of clarity here, I am using the term 'readers' to also include those who listen to audiobooks; in other words, all consumers of books, whether written or recorded).

Let's consider for a moment the type of people who read (and I'm specifically talking about non-fiction books like this one and the one you would write to grow your business):

- They are interested in self-improvement and have clear goals, whether that be fixing a problem, learning new strategies, learning overall, or enhancing a certain part of their life or business.
- They are happy to spend money on the aforementioned learning and self-improvement, as evidenced by their purchasing books.
- They are coachable and open to learning from experts in fields in which they have an interest, or they wouldn't be reading non-fiction.
- They're willing to invest time to acquire new skills and knowledge, rather than looking for a quick fix or shortcuts.
- They take active, conscious steps to progress and develop, since if they are buying and reading a book on a subject, they aren't procrastinating, delaying, or making excuses as to why they can't or shouldn't.

All of these traits, as I'm sure you must agree, go some way to separating the dreamier clients from clients we'd rather not work with in our businesses. By way of demonstrating this point, consider if the opposite traits were present in our clients:

- They don't want to improve or learn new things, and they have no goals in life or business.
- They are reluctant (or can't afford) to spend money on education and books.
- They aren't coachable, they believe they know exactly how things should be done, and they can't be guided.
- They don't feel like they're going to get value from a book, so they won't invest their time in reading one.
- They procrastinate, delay, make excuses, and never move forward.

Of course, there will be exceptions to this, such as if a high-level coach or entrepreneur wants to bypass the whole learning and implementation process by paying an expert for results and staying in their own zone of genius. I have worked with many clients like this—clients who would much rather pay me and my team to plan, ghostwrite, and publish their book for them, rather than learn about the process and apply the steps themselves. As a whole, however, targeting those who actively read and look to learn can never be a bad thing, because successful people tend to be readers, and vice versa.

This same point has been stated and reiterated, echoed, and emphasised many times over. Successful entrepreneurs across the world, such as Bill Gates, Jeff Bezos, Oprah Winfrey, and Richard Branson, have clearly expressed a passion for books, reading, and new knowledge. An article published by Forbes in 2022 proclaimed, 'Successful Leaders Are Avid Readers'.

With this said, attracting leads in the form of readers can never be a bad thing, as their characteristics mirror those of Dreamy Clients.

PERCEIVED AUTHORITY AND CREDIBILITY

When a business owner, entrepreneur, coach, mentor, thought leader, or speaker writes and publishes a book that takes their reader on a truly transformational journey, it's a given they are an expert in their field.

They are so committed to their craft that they have decided to write and publish a book on it. (Does this sound like you?)

They are experienced and well equipped enough to take you, the reader, on a journey of new insights, transformation, and results. (This definitely sounds like you!)

They aren't simply dabbling in their field. If they were, they wouldn't be able to share enough to warrant a full book. (If you're *dabbling*, maybe come back to this book when you're not...)

This is something your readers, whether consciously or subconsciously, will come to know about you when you publish a book. They'll know that you're clearly well versed in your field, that you have taken clients through a transformational journey, and that you have a skillset, experience, and the results to support everything you and your business can do for your clients. Otherwise, surely you wouldn't have been able to write a full, engaging book on the topic, leading your reader from problem to solution.

Case in point:

I once had a client who told me she wanted to write a book on an area she had newly discovered in her own life. Despite being successful in her business and the niche in which she was operating, she was considering writing a book on something she had quite literally stumbled across only days before and which was therefore completely new to her. While acknowledging the excitement she was feeling and her want to share with the world this amazing realisation she had had, I gently told her she wasn't experienced enough to be able to lead anyone—whether a reader or otherwise—on any transformational journey. Mere days don't make anyone an expert, and an author needs to be able to lead someone on a true journey of transformation (i.e. to move the reader farther away from their pain point) in order to qualify as an expert. She hadn't even lived that transformation for herself, let alone led anyone else through that experience, and she also wouldn't be able to showcase any results.

Essentially, she hadn't been on the journey herself, let alone leading a client through it, so she really wasn't qualified to even try guiding a reader.

Thankfully, my advice was taken on board. Had it not been, that book could never have been more than a pamphlet introducing readers to nothing more than the concept, or the bare bones of an idea.

Having both the knowledge and the experience in your chosen field to write a book and commit to taking that through to publication and distribution separates you from those who do not have these critical components in their armoury. Moreover, it also clearly communicates to your ideal audience that you aren't in this game with a short-term vision; you are committed to your craft, to achieving excellence, and to sharing your mission (your process, products, and/or services) with the world, as evidenced by the time and effort invested in writing a book and widening your net of impact. All of this will allow you to be viewed through a lens of authority and credibility.

SELF-QUALIFYING (AND -DISQUALIFYING) PROSPECTS

This is perhaps one of the benefits of a lead-generating book that excites me the most.

By directing your readers' attention to what your business provides in terms of services and results, the offer suite you have available (i.e. the scale of services and their respective price points), the results your clients can expect to achieve, how your clients need to show up to work with you, and how they can go about taking the next step, your readers will do one of two things: they will either disqualify themselves from working with you, or they will qualify themselves as an ideal fit. Both of these scenarios are nothing short of perfect for well-seasoned entrepreneurs with proven offers and reliable client results.

Let's consider the former of these two scenarios:

When your prospective client disqualifies themselves from working with you, they might do so for several different reasons, with this conclusion being reinforced at different points in the book. (Take my example above, where I clearly speak to those who may be *dabbling* and kindly suggest they revisit this project at a later date.) As another simplified example, it could be that you are a business coach whose Dreamy Clients are women who are already achieving consistent $10K months in their business. If this is clearly communicated throughout your book, any women not currently at that point in their journey will know they're not yet a fit, in which case they might simply 'put a pin' in working with you until they achieve that criterion.

In contrast, some readers will recognise themselves as a perfect fit for you and your services. Perhaps you have discussed your flagship service. Let's take my own book-writing and -publishing mastermind as an example. In this case, the reader would understand how the women enrolling need to be ready to move forward now, are hardcore action-takers and implementors, are kind, coachable, compassionate, and supportive, and understand that a five-figure investment is a complete no-brainer when it comes to writing and publishing an international bestselling book that can grow their business.

Of course, as a publishing professional, my thoughts on some aspects of these particular examples would be that if your title, subtitle, blurb, and overall marketing/messaging for your book are crafted in the right way, these would already rule out anyone not fitting this very basic Dream Client profile. Nonetheless, they highlight how your content can work for your and your business' benefit by having your readers self-identify as ideal or non-ideal.

Taking this a step further, what can realistically happen when your readers identify themselves as being a non-ideal fit? Well, the hope would be that they then wouldn't book into your calendar and use up the most valuable resource you have in your business: time. They also won't enrol into any of your programs and services they aren't a fit for (because, again, you've been very clear about who your content will and will not work for), meaning the chances of chargebacks and clients who don't make progress (and maybe even blame you for that) are so much lower.

On the other hand, imagine a reader self-identifying as a perfect fit for you...

Hayley's looking for women who want to write and publish a book now, no excuses. Yes, I'm ready to move now.

She wants women who know a five-figure investment is amazing value for this service. Yes, I definitely see that.

She wants women who can schedule in two hours every week to move the needle on this journey. I'll make it happen.

She wants clients who don't need to know the ins and outs of everything, but trust in the process. Just tell me where to sign up!

This is how it goes. And the real beauty of this? Not only do your services, masterminds, and high-level programs become filled with only the most amazing clients, but your team's resources are no longer being wasted.

Think no more call schedules full to bursting with half-non-fit prospects, wasting your sales team's time.

Think no more 'objection-handling'.

Think no more appalled expressions when you disclose the investment.

To me, this is the absolute epitome of business dreaminess.

RELATIONSHIP-BUILDING AT ITS FINEST

When I was first starting my entrepreneurial journey, I came across a female entrepreneur who specialised in helping women to scale a business. She spoke about how she'd once been in my position: worked to the point of exhaustion, her life whizzing by her in a blur, while she lived a life full of financial and time-related pressure as she pursued her professional passion.

After seeing this content and identifying myself as fitting her Ideal

Client profile, I enrolled into her $27 monthly academy. It was inside this program that I came to know Grace: her go-to catchphrases, her terms of endearment, and the way she moved and took action in her business. She was warm, funny, likeable, and down to earth.

I became a superfan overnight (and although she's no longer active in the online entrepreneurial space, I continue to be one, with so much gratitude for all she led me through).

What was really interesting to me was that after watching dozens of hours' worth of content and going away and silently implementing, I felt like I had a bond with Grace—and not just a one-way bond, but a mutual relationship. I knew her. And she knew me—or so it felt—because she was speaking *to me* in everything she was teaching.

In reality, of course, she didn't know I existed. The most she will have known at this point in my journey was that someone called Hayley Paige had enrolled into her academy and was moving through her program modules.

As I progressed on in my journey, however—as I did what she was teaching me to do, as I was watching the results snowball, and as my business was growing—I was soon able to uplevel and self-identify as a Dream Client, at which point I took the next steps to work with her in a closer capacity. I enrolled into a higher-level program and committed full steam ahead to my publishing company. It was at this point—some two years after initially developing my own relationship with Grace—that she came to actually know me and began developing the mutual side of our relationship!

One thing I regularly share with my 1:1 and mastermind clients is the need to be raw, real, and relatable. Show your readers who you are. Be vulnerable. Be human. Be transparent. If you commit to that, you'll very naturally be a magnet and attract those people who truly resonate with you and what you can help them to achieve, and the relationship will go from strength to strength.

It is this very same concept that provides one of the cornerstones of a lead-generating book:

As your readers move through your book, they will come to know you: the way you speak, the vocabulary you use, what matters to you, the difficulties you've navigated, how you view the world and your business, and your cause and mission.

They'll come to like you and all you represent, which commonly leads to them seeking to consume anything and everything you create and send out into the world.

And they'll come to trust you as you share the good *and* the bad; the client wins and the losses; the results you've achieved, and the realistic expectations your clients should have as they embark on their journey. Being authentic and transparent across all areas, speaking into the challenges and being sure you don't lead someone down the garden path—can be so valuable in building up trust.

Essentially, they will start to build a relationship with you right from the very beginning of your book—ideally, right from the Foreword (more on that in Chapter 7)—and you'll be completely oblivious. You'll be living your life and running your business as many people are coming to really, truly feel into who you are and build a relationship centred on the premise of know, like, and trust.

And if they don't know, like, and trust you after reading your book? Well, then they'll disqualify themselves from working with you, which is a complete win–win.

YOUR DISCOVERY CALLS IN A BOOK

When I share with my clients that your book can essentially negate the need for you and/or your team to get on sales calls, I won't lie: the moment of disbelief and awe is amazing.

As a rule of thumb, if you plan, write and publish your book in the right way, it can provide your prospects with all the information they could possibly need to make an informed decision as to whether they want to work with you going forward. Think about the information you regularly tend to provide to prospects on a sales, discovery or alignment call. I would wager much of it is the same; the walk-through of your services, the price points, the benefits, the bonuses, maybe even the cost of *not* working with you. Then moving on to the next steps, sending a proposal, payment plans and contracts. In other words, you or your team may very well be spending a great deal of time repeating the same content over and over again—and, really, who wants to do that when there's a better way?

That is to say, you can discuss the details of your programs and services, handle any objections, provide information on investment points, and answer commonly asked questions. This allows you, as a business owner, CEO or other professional, to focus your time on where it really needs to be spent and where you want it to be spent (think product creation, delivering the service, or doing whatever aligns with your dream vision of your business.

When I look at the many different calls I've spent my time on, I know so many of the same worries and concerns have arose:

I'm worried I won't have the time.
You need just seventeen minutes a day. Do you think you can free that up somewhere? It's just two hours a week.

I'm worried I'm not expert enough.
Do you help your clients get results? You're absolutely expert enough.

I'm good at speaking, but not writing.
Well, you can either opt for one of our ghostwriting solutions, or maybe just speak and transcribe your book...

And then there are so many of the same questions:

Will my book be made available on Amazon?
Yes, of course—Amazon is the biggest book retailer in the world! However, it's not the only one by far. We make our books available to thousands of distributors, wholesalers and retailers across the globe, so stores like Barnes & Noble, Chapters Indigo, Walmart, Target, Waterstones, Amazon and Kindle, to name a few leading retailers.

Do I need to pay for every book that's printed?
No, you will never need to pay outright for printing. Print costs and the retailer's cut come out of the RRP. The royalty remains—and you receive one hundred percent of that royalty.

Will I be able to get my book actually into book stores?
Absolutely. If a book store [manager] can see there is demand for your book, they'll be happy to physically stock it on their shelves. They just need to know the cost of shelf space is going to be recouped.

(See Client FAQs (page 225) for further questions commonly asked by my clients.)

Now, don't get me wrong: none of the questions or objections are invalid or come down to a lack of common sense or are a waste of time— quite the opposite—and I'm sure it's exactly the same for you. But that doesn't mean hearing yourself on repeat isn't frustrating, especially when there's a better, more effective, more efficient way of doing something. And, as wave-makers, shouldn't that always be the priority?

A TASTER OF YOUR RESULTS

If your book is focused on providing your readers with a taste of the results you can help them to achieve, you'll be turning cold readers into warm prospects.

In everything we do inside our publishing house, from teaching our clients how to outline and blueprint their book all the way through to helping them to launch their very own million-dollar publishing company, the one key element underpinning every single product and service is making sure they experience a transformational journey.

Your readers/prospects/Dreamy Clients need to be able to witness a transformation of some kind, no matter how big or small. If you can focus your attention on achieving this between the covers of your book, they will be far more likely to want to progress their relationship with you. Provide so much value that your readers emerge from your book with new knowledge, new skills, and true insights as to how they can move forward in a productive, quantifiable way. Provide results that they are left thinking, *If this is what she offers just in her book, what does her mastermind look like?*

One of my mastermind clients, Lisa (who we talked about in the Introduction), had this very same thought when she joined me earlier this year. She told me the following on a recorded interview:

> *I knew the standard of what you offer would be amazing, because I know you, but I was absolutely blown away when I got inside your mastermind. I realised then that everyone needs to see behind the curtain. Everyone needs to know about this.*
>
> *And if this is the value of your $20K program, I can't begin to imagine the value of your $250K program.*
>
> —LISA A. SMITH
> *'Retire by 45' Expert & Mentor*

(You can watch the interview here:
www.entrepreneurbooksuccess.com/interviews)

This sums up the thoughts, awe, and amazement we want your readers to be feeling. Help them to reduce the gap between where they are and where they want to be by providing a taste of your service and results, and you'll be warming them to the point that they won't ever want to consider working with anyone else but you.

ACTION STEPS: CHAPTER 2

1. Take a look at your bookshelf—whether physical or digital—and see if you can identify a dozen or so lead-generating/authority books written by professionals. Ask yourself: if they're doing this, surely there has to be a strategic reason?
2. Ingrain the benefits deep into your mind by writing down the following half-sentences—whether with good old-fashioned ink and paper, or on a tablet or virtual Notes app—and then completing the sentence in your own words:

- o Through a book, my leads will pay to become leads. This happens as a result of_____

  _____

  _____

- o Readers are dreamy prospects. I know this because readers are known to _____

  _____

  _____

- o Writing a book can help to enhance my perceived authority and credibility by _____

  _____

  _____

- o A book will mean by readers self-qualify (and even disqualify) themselves to work with me by _____

  _____

  _____

- o A book will allow me to build and nurture a relationship with my ideal readers. I can do this by _____

  _____

  _____

- o I can position my book to do my Sales, Discovery and/or Alignment calls for me/my team by _____

  _____

  _____

- o I can give my readers a taste of my products and/or services by _____

  _____

  _____

3. Watch the interview with Lisa A. Smith on the power of The Write and Publish Your Book Mastermind. This will allow you to feel completely supported as you undertake your book-writing journey: www.entrepreneurbooksuccess.com/interviews.

4. Share your key takeaways for Chapter 2 inside the Facebook group: www.facebook.com/groups/entrepreneurbooksuccess.

CHECKLIST: CHAPTER 2

1. Took stock of all lead-generating/authority books in my library and fully ingrained how valuable these books must be to the authors and their businesses.
2. Ingrained the benefits deep into my mind by writing down all of the key benefits and how I personally and professionally can grow using a book.
3. Watched the interview with Lisa A. Smith.
4. Shared my key takeaways for Chapter 2 inside the Facebook group.

CHAPTER 3
BOOK = BOOKED

THE ONLY LIMIT TO OUR REALISATION OF
TOMORROW WILL BE OUR DOUBTS TODAY.

—FRANKLIN DELANO ROOSEVELT (1882–1945)
President of the United States

IF YOU WRITE A LEAD-GENERATING book and you do it well (again: if you do it *well*), your book has the power to generate leads and nurture them into your business forevermore.

Not only that, but if the know, like, and trust has been created and built on, and if your readers emerge from the book with huge takeaways and clear steps regarding what they need to do next, your book can actually work for you in your business (like an employee would), even when you don't.

It's also critical that your book's publication standards reflect the standards you align yourself with in your business and in the provision of your products/services, but more on this in Chapter 10: Routes to Publication.

More so, your lead-generating book can be unbelievably powerful in building a relationship with your reader—a relationship you're completely oblivious to as it's being nurtured—and in moving that relationship 'off the page' (into your business).

Essentially, a book can mean you and your company being flooded with hot leads, because your readers have had a taste of what you offer and have seen the results for themselves. This opens the way for your business to be booked to capacity, whatever that looks like for you (you get to choose).

It might mean just a handful of new clients every month and a growing waiting list, because that's what you've decided you want.

It might mean throwing rocket fuel on your business' growth and expanding to meet demand: more staff, more premises, and exponential expansion.

Whatever your goals and whatever business-related success looks for you, it's achievable with a book. First, though, you need to set the stage for an 'off the page' relationship and do things in the right way—and to do that, there are five key components: tell people you can be booked; show you can be booked; communicate that you're not out of reach; have your readers qualify or disqualify themselves as Ideal Clients; and move those self-qualified readers into an 'off the page' relationship. Each of these is discussed here.

THE FIVE KEY COMPONENTS TO GOING FROM 'BOOK' TO 'BOOKED'

COMPONENT 1: TELL PEOPLE YOU CAN BE BOOKED

The first rule: if you don't tell people what your services look like and how they can go about working with you, you won't get booked. It's as simple as that. Yes, your readers can do their own research, seek you out, look you up on social media, and send DMs and emails, but do you want that for them? Do you want them to have to chase their tail and spend their most valuable resource (time) on something you could have made so much simpler? Of course not. If you want your readers—who have become warmed, nurtured superfans who have tasted your expertise and witnessed transformation just through your book—to take the next steps, you need to provide them with those steps.

I don't mean explicitly 'selling to' your readers. That's an absolute no-no. Your readers haven't invested their time and energy into your book so they can be pitched to. They don't want to be snuggled down into a chair and immersed in your book, only to be told they need your six-figure, six-month intensive 1:1 coaching in order to get any 'real' progress. No. But they do need to know that there are more steps available to them, should they want to take this journey further.

COMPONENT 2: SHOW, DON'T TELL

The key, for the most part, is to *show* that you can be booked and that your services can be secured, rather than *tell*. This means sharing your clients' wins and successes; the little anecdotes that are essentially underpinned by what you do in your business and the service you provided to said client. This not only provides your readers with the knowledge that you do have, for example, a mastermind or a retreat or a self-guided program, but it also piques their interest and forces them to visualise whether this could work for them.

'A mastermind? That sounds like the support I'd need!'

'A retreat? Ooh, I can imagine going on a book-writing retreat!'

'A self-guided program? I'd love to make progress at my own pace!'

Remember: it's critical we give our readers all the tools they need to progress in their journey, and that includes information pertaining to paid and high-ticket next steps. You don't force it down their throats, but you do subtly allude to what's available, should they feel aligned with the results you offer (as showcased by your client anecdotes) and the way in which the results are achieved (mastermind, 1:1 mentoring, etc.).

Of course, this isn't always possible, and it's absolutely fine to *tell* at times, too. But, where you can, showcase your clients, make them look good, and the rest will follow.

COMPONENT 3: YOU ARE NOT OUT OF REACH

I remember an alignment call I once had with a really lovely woman early in 2023. Let's call her Emma. Emma and I had known each other for a handful of years after spending some time together in the inner circle of my very first mentor, Grace (more about that later in this chapter). Fast-forward four years, and Emma was finally ready to discuss writing her book.

When we hopped onto the call, Emma shared with me how she had never taken the step to work with me because she had been under the impression that I worked only with celebrities, famous people, and millionaires. I questioned how she had arrived at that conclusion (which couldn't have been further from the truth) and quickly corrected her: my 'Dream Client' criteria had nothing to do with status, celebrity, notoriety, fame, or money. It was all about them being ready now to take action and hold themselves accountable; about them being driven, goals-focused, kind, and compassionate.

What I took away from that conversation was that some people were viewing me as 'out of reach', and when I discussed this with one of my mentors, she agreed that other people in our circle had been under that same false impression.

Cue my feeling horrified that some of the women I had been wanting to work with might have ruled themselves out!

This one call, which took place years and years into me running my business, taught me that we need to be very clear about who we work with and what that looks like (and also who we *don't* work with). If we're not clear on this or we think something 'goes without saying', we could be missing out on a pool of Dream Clients.

So, with this lesson under my belt, I will emphasise a few things here, in the context of your book:

- It really doesn't matter if your title and/or subtitle is crafted to call in only your Dreamy Clients (and by the way, your publisher should see to it that that's the case). Even if you have the very best title and subtitle combination, who your Dreamy Clients are needs to be stated and repeated throughout your book.
- It really doesn't matter if you've been clear in your blurb about the type of clients you work with (and, again, your publisher should see to it that that's the case). Even if you have the very best blurb, the type of clients you work with needs to be stated and repeated throughout your book.
- It really doesn't matter if you've mentioned in your Introduction what your Dreamy Clients look like (once again, your editor should see to it that that's the case). Even if you have the very best

Introduction, what your Dreamy Clients look like needs to be stated and repeated throughout your book.

COMPONENT 4: QUALIFY AND DISQUALIFY

This leads beautifully from Component 3 and is perhaps one of the things I love most about lead-generating authority books: the fact that we can lead our clients through either qualifying themselves to work with us or disqualifying themselves. Both are worth untold amounts of revenue for your business.

When I talk to people about the power of a book in their business, this tends to be one of my go-to points: your readers either qualify or disqualify themselves for working with you in a real-life, real-world, high-touch situation, and what's so beautiful about this is that it doesn't mean any kind of loss for your business.

First, let's consider how your book can qualify your Dreamy Clients:

Through subtle anecdotes and storytelling (whether your own experiences in your business or the experiences of your clients and how they've shown up), you can be very clear about what you need from your clients in order for them to be a good fit for you, and what you offer.

As an example: one of my really amazing clients, Jamie, who is a busy mother and entrepreneur working in real estate, came across a post I had written in an online group. Despite having countless plates spinning (renovating and selling properties, being present for her son, continuing her own education, and pursuing professional licenses), she decided she absolutely had to reach out to me to start her book-writing journey. Jamie saw just one piece of my content and, upon hearing the little voice inside her head that told her to start her book journey, she acted.

When the right person was identified by the universe and put right in her path, Jamie didn't miss a beat. She followed me on social media, added me as a contact, requested access to my free Facebook group, sent me a message, asked for details on my services, asked how she could start, and signed up as a client—all within twenty-four hours.

Jamie didn't allow busyness or parenting or entrepreneurship or education or life's general happenings to stop her from taking bold, courageous action, because she knew life is life, and life is always busy, especially when we throw business and children into the mix. That's a whole vibe I can get behind, not only because I move in exactly the same way, but because I've seen how showing up with that kind of energy and massive action tends to lead to radical success.

You'd be forgiven for thinking the busiest clients would struggle to make the most progress and achieve the most wins, but in my experience, the opposite is true: those who take action quickly and show up despite full schedules tend to quantum leap time and time again. In contrast, it seems to be the most fearful (not the most time-starved) who don't make progress.

Note: by highlighting the way in which Jamie and I met (and, specifically, how Jamie showed up for me as a prospective client and then as a Dreamy Client), my readers know that being a fast-moving action-taker is something I really love and appreciate. By that same token, if they recognise themselves as being procrastinators or excuse-makers, or as people who regularly say things like, 'I'd love to, but...', they're probably not going to fit my Dreamy Client profile. In other words, they can self-disqualify for my services.

This qualification process can run throughout your book, and it very intentionally separates those who would be perfect for your most high-level services and those who are better suited to self-guided programs, for example—not to mention those who don't fit the 'Dreamy Client' profile at all. If you're able to do this in your day-to-day business marketing and messaging, you can absolutely do it in a book.

I am very intentional about this when people are considering scheduling a call for my mastermind, as an example. I state very clearly how I want 'kind' and 'coachable' women inside my mastermind—women who are ready to write their books *now*. In other words, I don't want rudeness. I don't want those who can't be guided. I don't want procrastinators. I don't want people who reach out, make moves, and then ghost.

So, be clear about this in your book. Talk about the results you've achieved for your clients. Talk about what your programs and services look like. Talk about the time investment. Allude to your price points. All of this will really help your readers to look at themselves and question whether they're a good fit for you and whether they're truly ready to act now, because nobody wants to waste their resources (whether time, energy, or money).

Be your true self and show your business for what it really is. Don't water it down. Again, you want your non-Ideal Clients to disqualify themselves.

They don't like you? Great, they won't come into your business.

They think your services are overpriced? Amazing, they won't book calls and waste your business resources.

They think you swear too much? Fabulous, they won't sign up for group calls.

It's all a win. It either allows you to create incredibly aligned superfans for your business who you will enjoy working with and helping every step of the way (and who will, of course, generate revenue into your business), or it will save everyone a whole lot of time, stress, and struggle in the form of wasted time on calls, or, worse, inevitable refunds.

Consider the stories you can tell—the wins you can share and the clients you can reference—and allow the story to *show* your readers what you need them to know. The rest will very naturally come together.

COMPONENT 5: CALL-TO-ACTIONS

It's incredibly important that by the end of your book, your reader knows exactly what they need to do to move forward with you in a real-life relationship. I'm not talking subtle references (which are sprinkled throughout your book and which ultimately provide your reader with the time and freedom to casually research or nonchalantly follow you on social media); I'm talking about the very intentional, very proactive next steps that guide them to their next level of success.

It's essential that when you're leading your readers on a transformational journey, your sole focus is on providing value. At the end of the book, however, your role with regards sharing value is to share exactly how your reader can experience *more*: more transformation, more results, and more of you.

This is where you truly take your client from 'book' to 'booked'.

To be clear, your book can and should include subtle references for how someone can find, approach, and work with you, but at the end of the book, there is no time or room for subtlety. Be clear.

Providing a Resources page at the back of the book is one of the most valuable, simple, and easy ways of providing your readers with what they need to do to further their journey (see Chapter 7: What to Include and What *Not* to Include). However, as some people (albeit a small proportion) won't read the Resources page (and as we want to serve as many of our readers as possible by giving them the tools they need to make as much progress as possible), we want to be more direct in the body of the book—specifically, in the final chapter.

It is in your final words to your reader that you want to be very clear on what they can do to enhance their transformation and achieve even bigger things going forward.

Look at my closing chapter as an example. There is no dillydallying:

I tell my readers (you!) what they should do if they want to start blueprinting and outlining their book.

I tell them what they should do if they've already written a first draft and want professional publication.

I tell them what their next steps should be if they want to outsource the project and hire me as their ghostwriter.

I tell them what they should do if they want to go all in and widen their net of impact in the biggest possible way by launching their own publishing house.

I speak into all of that, very clearly and very directly, because I *want* my readers to be successful. I *want* my readers to decide they really, truly want and need to write a book and now, and for them to not be able to believe that they've waited so long. I want them to think, *How much money have I been leaving on the table all this time?!* I want that thought to be at the forefront of my readers' minds. I don't want a casual, lackadaisical attitude ('Yeah, I'll maybe perhaps do it one day, possibly next year or maybe never, but it's just not a priority right now...') as they place the book on a shelf and then trundle through life and business. No! I want momentum to be growing and for this amazing transformation to be continued in a setting that is far more conducive for achieving the big goals. To do anything else is to do a disservice to your reader—to the time, energy, and money they've invested in you and your book. They've turned to you for direction, expertise, and help, so you have to be sure to do this for them.

AN 'OFF THE PAGE' RELATIONSHIP

By incorporating all five of these components into your book, you'll be better positioned to move your reader from your book to your business and into an 'off the page' relationship with you. This is where the real magic happens; where everything that falls beyond the scope of your book can be covered in the greatest possible detail, with no limit.

I have seen the power of this both as a client myself and also in my professional role. Sadly, however, I've also watched the opposite unfold, like car crash TV, with a book completely failing to do its job, simply because the author didn't incorporate everything they needed to.

To speak into the former: in 2017, when I signed with my very first mentor, I signed up for a self-guided program. As mentioned earlier, I was learning the ins and outs of delivering high-level solutions within the boundaries of the entrepreneurial world, and I was feeling lost.

Cue me diving feet-first into a program that gave me the preliminary steps I needed to move through to achieve my first goals.

What was really special to me during this time was that Grace, with her pre-recorded video, was allowing me to feel seen, understood, and, most importantly, empowered. Through her teachings, I was developing know like, and trust. I was forming a relationship with her (albeit a parasocial one), and truth be told, I was in complete awe of her. She was kind and sweet, supportive and encouraging, and she made me feel like I could do and achieve anything.

I forged onward and achieved everything she said I could—and so a superfan was born.

Of course, when I reflect, I think how amazing this is, because at that point in time, Grace had no clue I existed. Maybe she'd seen my name on a payment that came through, and maybe she saw I was on her email list. Both of those things are possible. But I wasn't in her world—not her real-life, real-business world. Not at that point. I was just another 'someone' consuming her program content, experiencing a huge transformation, developing know, like, and trust, and becoming so sold on what she was delivering that I absolutely had to take the next steps.

And I did. I went on to become a very active, very prominent client in her circle. I went on to become a client inside her inner circle, enrolled in intensive trainings, attended a retreat at her home in Adelaide, Australia, and spoke onstage at her Los Angeles event in 2019. I moved quickly and actively, from a self-guided program to high-touch work, because I'd developed a relationship with her—all while she was none the wiser.

Why is this relevant? Because your book will work in exactly the same way. As you read these words now, am I, the author, aware? No. Am I aware of how invested you are in the process? Probably not. Do I even know your name? Not if my book is doing its job properly!

This will continue to happen now and forever, because that's how these books work. Very naturally, your readers will move through the book, digesting the content, learning and implementing, seeing progress unfold before their very eyes, and getting to know you, how you work, what resonates with you, what doesn't resonate with you, and how you love your clients to show up in your work together. All of that culminates to create a bond—a relationship—and the natural next step after they reach the end of the book is taking that relationship to the next level.

As evidence of this, aren't you slightly curious, at this point, about what it might feel like to move into a container with me? To have me and my team guiding you across this journey and into this whole new world of uplevelling? It's a natural progression.

Sadly, though, I have known authors who, quite simply, have been unaware of what a lead-generating book should do, what its purpose is, and how it's essentially a means of demonstrating your value: leading your client further away from pain and closer to resolution, and then *into your business*. I provide an example of this in Chapter 7.

What is perhaps even harder to swallow is when I've worked with clients who are very stuck in their ways and who won't budge or take advice, despite the fact that they've hired an expert to help them (this is why I'm very clear now about wanting only 'coachable' clients!).

There have been times when a client hasn't wanted to consider changing the working title and subtitle they have come up with (and subsequently become married to), even if it means negatively impacting the discoverability and therefore sales of their book.

There have been clients who use incorrectly spelled words, or words in the wrong context, and then dig their heels in: that version absolutely must go to publication (side note: although our clients maintain creative control, I cannot ever align myself with publishing works that undermine our business reputation).

All these things break my heart a little, because I know the power of a book in your business *if it's done in the right way*. I'm so invested in every single client's success that I want to see every book live out its full potential, so that it can allow the entrepreneur in front of me to write and publish books they can be proud of and that can help their business to grow and flourish. Only then can they truly embody the premise that is 'Book = Booked'.

ACTION STEPS: CHAPTER 3

1. Share your key takeaways for Chapter 3 inside the Facebook group: www.facebook.com/groups/entrepreneurbooksuccess.

CHECKLIST: CHAPTER 3

1. Shared my key takeaways for Chapter 3 inside the Facebook group.

CHAPTER 4
GETTING CLEAR ON THE FIGURES

DON'T SIT DOWN AND WAIT FOR THE OPPORTUNITIES
TO COME. GET UP AND MAKE THEM.

—MADAM C. J. WALKER (1867–1919)
Entrepreneur, Philanthropist, and Political and Social Activist

WHEN MAKING ANY FINANCIAL DECISIONS, it is of course super-important to be clear on what the return on investment looks like. In some cases, financial ROI isn't overly relevant, as the intangible results and benefits might be ROI enough, but when it comes to a book, this one factor alone makes the entire process a complete no-brainer, especially when comparing a book with other lead-generating approaches.

As entrepreneurs, we are regularly introduced and exposed to many different marketing and advertising approaches, whether paid ads, conversational marketing, interacting in social media groups, or even running free challenges and webinars—not to mention sending out regular lengthy email campaigns. And in that same vein, the subject of conversions is a key metric:

How many calls do you need to have with prospective clients for every 'close'?

How many emails do you need to send out to generate $10,000?

How much needs to be invested in ad spend for you to acquire x amount of new leads and y amount of new clients?

How much is your cost per lead?

As with any other marketing tool, the same calculation needs to be completed for your book. So, let's take a look at the figures.[1,2]

EXAMPLE 1: LET'S TALK COLD CONVERSIONS

As entrepreneurs and business owners, we know that as a baseline average, we can expect between 1%-3% of a cold audience to buy into our offers. For the sake of being both conservative and realistic (especially while you might be having thoughts of, *Can a book really add* x *amount to my business revenue?),* we'll assume 2% of your cold audience are the type to take action.

So, let's imagine introducing your book to your new email subscribers and social media followers through a series of emails and posts. We can then realistically and conservatively expect to generate sales of your book amounting to 2% of your cold email list and new social media network.

For the sake of simplicity, let's say the new subscribers on your email list total 1,000 (not a significant email list), while those on your social media who are connected but don't know you well total 4,000. With these numbers, you could expect to generate twenty sales from email and eighty from social media. That's a total of 100—meaning 100 valuable leads.

Why are they valuable? Because despite being 'cold' mere moments before, they have taken a look at your book and its intentionally crafted title and subtitle, read its description/blurb (which communicates who the book is for and what it will help those readers achieve), and identified themselves as needing whatever expertise you share in your book.

---

[1] For the sake of the examples provided here, I'm going to assume your book has all of the must-have pieces not only in place, but completed to a high standard. These include all the components needed to position your book for success as the very best version of itself. See Chapter 7.

[2] When discussing average opt-in and purchase percentages, I will be taking a simplified approach. Of course, this very subject matter could span an entire series, and to discuss this in-depth would fall beyond the scope of this book. As such, in these examples, I'll be considering average percentages.

Let's just take a moment to pause and reflect on that last part: those leads have recognised they need your book and have taken a step to get the help they need—i.e. they have ordered your book (most notably owing to the way in which the title and subtitle have been crafted, leading your reader to self-qualify).

It is at this stage in the journey your reader is recognising they are in a hole and your book is their ladder.

A good start—and at this point, I would hope a little spark of excitement is going to swirl inside you, because if people on your email and social media lists are essentially looking at a product that helps them to get started with solving the problem you help them to solve, they are, in effect, raising their hand and telling you they want to start moving forward. Amazing!

Back to the example:

You've sold 100 copies of your book. Let's say that provides $400 in royalties. Not a bad amount of money to have generated from a couple of simple email blasts and a handful of social media posts—but, then again, you're probably the type of entrepreneur who charges that for an hour's work (assuming you even do charge by the hour), so does $400 really cover the time you've invested in planning and writing the book? Does it cover the investment required to publish? Maybe even the investment to have the book ghostwritten? Of course not; those royalties wouldn't come *close* to covering the time and financial investment involved (even with our 100% royalties publication service).

But that's the thing: royalties don't even factor when it comes to getting clear on the figures. These are just pennies compared to your book's true potential.

I know... It sounds crazy.

During my time spent on hundreds of discovery calls and explaining the figures underpinning a successful lead-generating book, I have seen many confused faces when I've made this very same statement, because we've all been led to believe that profiting from a book is near impossible: we'd each have to sell thousands of units to even break even! Honestly, the relief I see in my clients when I explain how things actually work is incredible. But more on that shortly.

So, you've sold 100 copies of your book, notably all to self-qualifying prospects (those people who have acknowledged they have the problem you help to solve and are ready—even if in some small way—to start moving forward and farther away from that pain point). So, now, let's examine what it could look like for your business if some of those 100 customers were to go one step further and opt into your paid services.

Again, as entrepreneurs familiar with opt-in rates versus close rates, as a simple average, we know to expect cold traffic to close at a rate of approximately 2%. So, even if we were to proceed with the view that everyone who has bought your book is cold (which we know they aren't, because they've already become a customer), we can then reasonably expect that 2% of those 100 prospects (a total of two clients) will buy into the high-ticket services discussed and detailed in your book.

Let's assume your high-ticket service is $5,000; that equates to $10,000 in new sales for your business because of your book—and from a cold audience. And if your high-ticket is $10,000, of course you're then generating $20,000.

So, again, I pose the question: does $20,000 cover the time you've invested in planning and writing the book? Does it provide a return on investment on publishing? The investment to have the book ghostwritten?

We're definitely getting closer, but we're still not quite there.

EXAMPLE 2: WARM CONVERSIONS

In contrast to the 2% average of cold traffic conversions, when it comes to *warm* traffic, we know the conversion is more likely to be around the 5% mark (although other well-known marketers in the space, such as Mike Shreeve, suggest it can be closer to the 10% mark, but let's stick with conservative and comfortable). This means, of the 5,000 leads reach, we can instead anticipate 250 copies being bought by our 1,000-strong *warm* email list and 4,000-strong *warm* social media list, with 12 (5%) of those 250 readers opting into higher ticket services.

To mirror the example of a $10,000 high-ticket service, these 12 clients equate to $120,000 in new revenue for every 250 books sold to warm contacts—and that's without taking into consideration the fact that some of those readers may also buy into the lower-ticket services detailed in your book, whether a $27 roadmap or detailed spreadsheet, a $197 masterclass or workshop, or a $1,997 program, for instance. It also doesn't take into account those readers that become leads that are later nurtured into clients, such as through email nurture.

With this example alone, I would state pretty definitively that $120,000 would absolutely cover the investment associated with actually getting your book crafted and sent out into the world. This applies regardless of whether you've written the book yourself and procured a turnkey publishing solution, or brain-dumped your book and handed it over to a team of experts for Hybrid Ghostwriting™ and publication—or even if you've gone the full ghostwriting and publication route. Whichever option, you're in profit from just one email blast and a couple of social media posts.

Now let's make things really exciting...

Imagine having a larger email list or social media network, or doing a speaking event and upselling your book as a result:

Email list of 5,000 and Social Media Network of 5,000 = 10,000 contacts

10,000 contacts @ 5% conversion = 500 books sold

500 books sold @ 5% conversion = the expectation that 25 readers will become high-ticket clients

25 high-ticket @ $10,000 = $250,000.

(Not to mention the additional $2,000 that would come from the royalties of selling 500 copies. But even considering without royalties, with a well-crafted book, with the perfect blend of lead-generation, you could even give your book away and still make money for your business. This is why we carefully bake subtle lead-generation into every book we publish.)

To provide a visual, your stream would look something like the diagram on the following page:

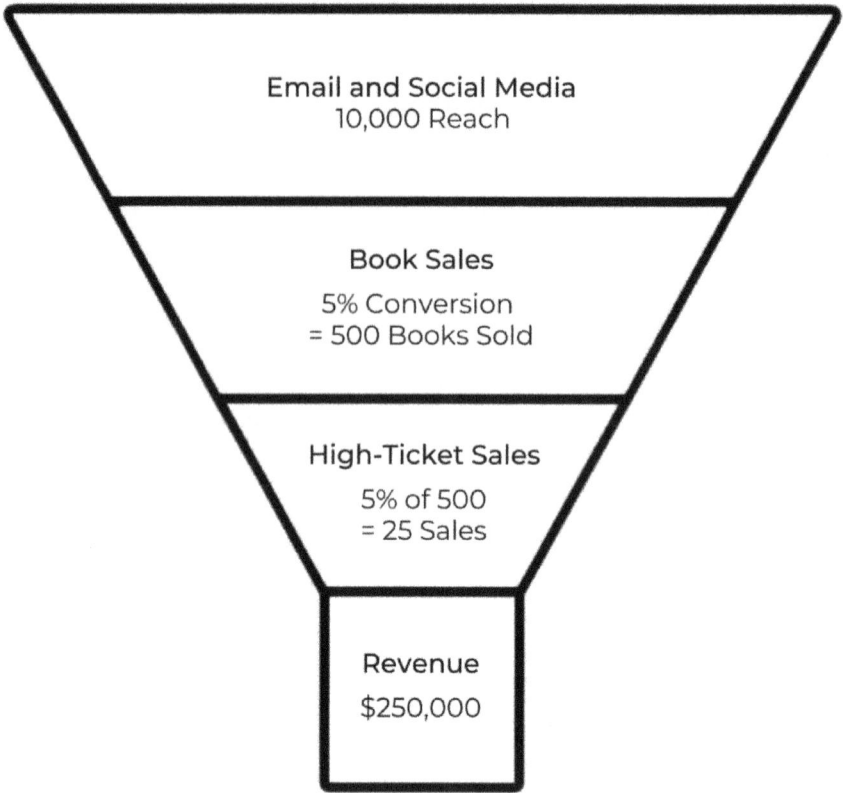

Figure 1:
Expected Revenue from Campaigns to 10,000 Contacts

So, with all of this considered, now would be a perfect (and really exciting) time for you to look at what the above could look like for you and your business.

Email list + Social Media Reach = number of contacts

Number of Contacts x 5% = number of books sold

Number of Books Sold x 5% = number of clients

Number of Clients x Service Price = Expected Revenue

Furthermore, in the case that your high-ticket service is actually $15,000, you can then expect those 25 new clients to collectively bring $375,000 into your business—not $250,000.

And for high-ticket services around the $50,000 mark, those 25 new clients will provide a revenue flow of $1.25 million.

To provide an accurate, real-life, real-business example, my own book leading people into our publishing house can expect to achieve the following:

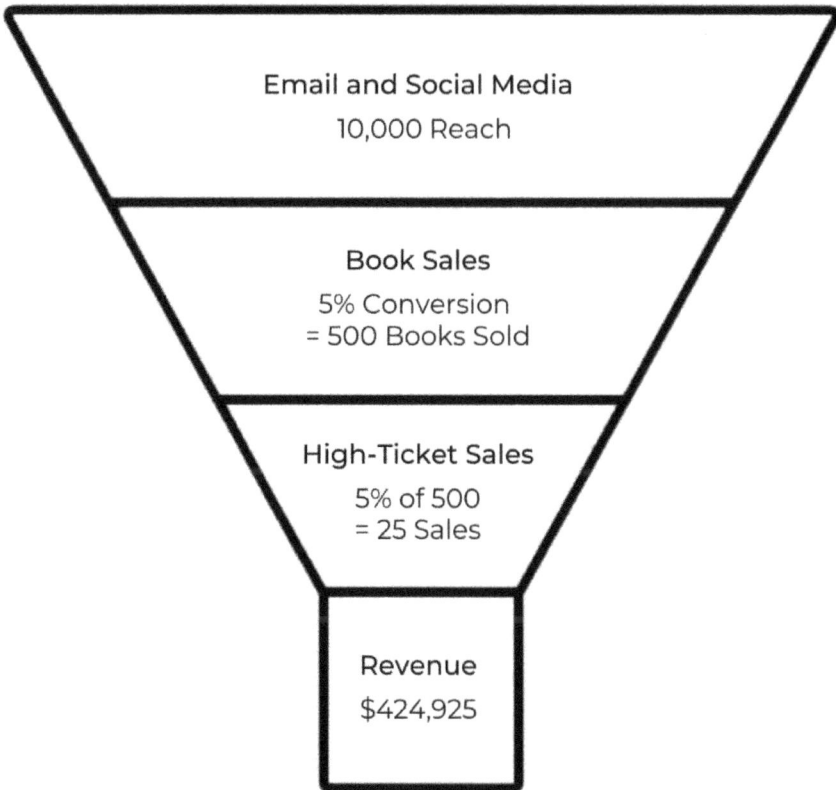

Email and Social Media
10,000 Reach

Book Sales
5% Conversion
= 500 Books Sold

High-Ticket Sales
5% of 500
= 25 Sales

Revenue
$424,925

Figure 2:
Projected Revenue Generated from *Entrepreneur. Book. Success.*
for Every 10,000 Contacts

And this is assuming those twenty-five clients choose our publication solution, not our higher-level solutions of Hybrid or Complete Ghostwriting (not to mention those clients opting for our *crème de la crème* solution of launching their own publishing house).

So, let me ask again: do you feel this level of revenue-generation would cover the time invested in planning and writing the book and having it professionally published and distributed?

At this point, I'm hoping you'll be desperate to get started, because the examples truly speak for themselves—even if you were to remove the burden of time by enlisting the professional help and expertise of a ghostwriter *and* publishing company. Even then, you'd be injecting your business with huge influxes of revenue, with incredible scope to continue repeating the cycle every single time you bring new people into your orbit.

UNLIMITED POTENTIAL

The really beautiful thing about this is that as your email/contact lists grow through any of the other avenues you commonly utilise in your business (whether organic traffic, webinars, funnels, and so on), you can continue to direct people to your book. This gives new followers the opportunity to come to learn about what you do; to raise their hand with the recognition that they need your expertise and get to know you and your services.

Imagine attending or running an event or being invited into a speaking opportunity, and at the end directing people to your book. Those people will be so warm and so invested in *you* that taking the next step in their journey with you will feel like a complete no-brainer.

For you to promote your book with the calculated, clear-on-the-figures expectation that every 250 copies that land in the hands of warm prospects has the potential to generate hundreds of thousands—if not millions—for your business, is absolutely incredible (even if you were to give your book away).

The potential is honestly out of this world. Mind-blowing. I say it every single day.

To conclude, when you get clear on the figures—and, moreover, when you actually see this working in your business—you'll wish you'd taken this step sooner and with greater urgency. You'll wish you'd seen how lucrative a book can be as a well-considered, strategic move in your business.

I will never forget what my investment coach and mentor, Lisa Smith, told me when we began working together in 2022: 'There's going to come a time, not too long in the future, when you're going to look back on this investment opportunity and say, "I wish I'd bought more."' Sure enough, within a few short months, I was wishing I'd invested even more into what was a golden opportunity.

Albeit a different context, that same golden opportunity is being presented here...

I guarantee it; you'll look back on your decision to write and publish a book and, although forever grateful for taking the leap when you did, you'll wish you'd done it sooner.

This same point was echoed during an interview with one of my very good clients, Jessa Bellman. A successful digital creator and Etsy™ mentor, Jessa first worked with me on a multi-author project in 2021. Loving this little taster experience of our service, she took the initiative to undertake her own lead-gen book project and proceeded to dive straight into 1:1 support inside our Mastermind and Publication solution.

During her interview, Jessa shared how she really wishes she had started sooner:

> That's my only regret. I really wish I could go back and tell myself to jump earlier and start years ago! I wish I'd started when we first met! And if I could speak to [everyone] in your circle, I'd be telling them to just go for it, because they'll be so glad they did!

This insight hit Jessa very early on in the process—way before her book was even written. Only three 1:1 sessions in, she had already achieved a huge return on investment and, shortly after, went on to land an amazing opportunity as a direct result of the strategies taught inside the mastermind (more on this in Chapter 13).

> That strategy is gold. And from a monetary point of view, it's bringing business into my business. Honestly, that one thing has changed the game.

I'm in surplus already, and the book's not even published yet.

(You can watch the interview here:
www.entrepreneurbooksuccess.com/interviews)

And that's honestly what's so truly incredible about using a book to grow your business. There's just no telling what opportunities will present themselves and what different streams of revenue will activate and pour into your business as a direct result of you being strategic enough to get clear on the figures and incorporate a book into your business.

AND... [HOT OFF THE PRESS]

To further showcase the true financial power of a book, I am incorporating this section of this chapter as a very last-minute, high-value addition to the book.

For the sake of transparency, I am sat writing this on August 5, 2023, as the rain pours relentlessly outside our publishing house office windows in the picturesque village of Bakewell, Derbyshire, the sky grey. You wouldn't believe we're in the thick of British summertime.

With the publication date set for in only a couple of weeks' time, we went to pre-order with this very book weeks ago, and since then have been directing our efforts to pre-launch marketing while I continue to write, as discussed in my note to my readers (Page 25). (Inside our publishing house, this is known as The Detour; where we guide our clients on planning their book, then going to pre-order before the book is even written.) With this noted, recent developments warrant sharing this real-time, very exciting development.

Just a few days ago, on August 2, 2023, *Entrepreneur. Book. Success.* generated $15,000 into our business. This came as a result of me sharing a sneak-peek of the book with one of our clients. She was so impressed with what she saw that she immediately sent me a DM and requested an upgrade to her service.

I want my book to be 'great', just like this. You've nailed it. You've completely nailed it. You are amazing at what you do. How do I upgrade?

Just like that.

She then asked that we send her a payment link, which was settled immediately.

What made this situation even more amazing is the fact that not only is this client a particularly Dreamy Client—fast-acting, an implementor, and a 'trust the process' and 'feel the fear and do it anyway' type—but that this led to yet another additional opportunity:

When sharing this development on social media, I was contacted and offered a writing opportunity that would allow me to showcase both this book *and* our publishing company to 85,000 coaches, mentors, and entrepreneurs—our Ideal Client base. And it would be completely reasonable to expect *that* opportunity to snowball and result in yet more business growth: more followers, more email subscribers, more warm leads, and, ultimately, more clients wanting to work with us. Why? Because although those 85,000 professionals might never have heard of me or our business, we know to expect 2% (1,700) of a cold audience to buy the book and 2% of those readers (34) to become clients moving forward. (Feel free to reach out to find out how it's been going!)

In short, that one opportunity could end up generating more than $650,000 for our business—and that's a conservative figure. Imagine just one of those clients wanting to move forward with launching their own successful book publishing company, and that adding an additional six figures to the potential.

I'll just let that percolate...

TO CONCLUDE

The most important thing to remember when it comes to the revenue-earning potential of your book? It's sales *from* the book, not sales *of* the book. Repeat after me:

It's sales *from* the book, not sales *of* the book.

Stay focused on this throughout your book-writing and -publication journey, and you'll feel motivated to prioritise making progress every single day.

It's the figures like those discussed in this chapter that provide huge motivation and inspiration for the likes of Grant Cardone, Maria Forleo, Russell Brunson, and Natalie Dawson (to name a few) to write and publish books. I'm sure these projects aren't undertaken for the sheer love of it (well, very rarely), but rather because high-level entrepreneurs know and understand that books are an incredible way of nurturing warm, dreamy prospects into their business and getting closer to staggering results.

It is my hope that just the very simple examples provided here inspire you and highlight the too-good-to-miss revenue-based benefits you and your business can expect to reap if you write and publish a book.

Try it for yourself.

This is only scratching the surface, but it should help you to see the bucketloads of potential—and it should also help you to understand why waiting until next year or 'a better time' quite simply makes no sense.

Don't believe me? Why not test the waters and tell your audience you are thinking of writing a book to help them? Be prepared for the response; you'll see for yourself.

People need your book.

ACTION STEPS: CHAPTER 4

1. Total up how many active email subscribers and social media contacts you have, and work out how many (5%) of them you can expect to order your book.
2. Calculate how many (5%) of those ordering your book you can expect to move forward into your higher-level solutions.
3. Calculate how much revenue this equates to in your business.
4. Watch the interview with Jessa Bellman on the power of The Write and Publish Your Book Mastermind. This will allow you to feel completely supported as you undertake your book-writing journey: www.entrepreneurbooksuccess.com/interviews.

5. Share your epiphanies, thoughts, and breakthroughs on Chapter 4 (and even the figures, if you feel so inclined) inside the Facebook group.

CHECKLIST: CHAPTER 4

1. Got clear on the figures.
2. (Got really bloody excited at the figures!)
3. Watched the interview with Jessa Bellman.
4. Shared your thoughts and breakthroughs on Chapter 4 inside the Facebook group.

PART II:
BOOK

CHAPTER 5
WHERE TO BEGIN

A PERSON WHO NEVER MADE A MISTAKE NEVER TRIED
ANYTHING NEW.

—ALBERT EINSTEIN (1879–1955)
Theoretical Physicist

THE VERY FIRST STARTING POINT to your book-writing journey is clearly outlining your book's concept—or, in other words, the type of book you want to write.

It is very common for my clients to feel like they have a ton of different ideas for different books they want to write, and this lends the way to action-halting overwhelm, since they can't decide *which* book they should write first. It's also super-common for me to speak with clients who aren't altogether convinced they have enough information, knowledge, or expertise to write the book they feel called to write.

With so many different clients voicing similar thoughts as they play with the idea of writing a book, I decided they needed something to give them a bit of a direction; a roadmap, essentially. So, inside my blueprinting program and mastermind, I devised a super-simple but effective strategy known as the 'Experience = Books Audit' to help them identify which book would be a no-brainer to write first.

Now, it's really important for me to highlight at this point that it might be that you already know exactly what book you want to write, including the different pain points you want to address and the journey you want to take your reader on, and that's absolutely fine. However, in the interest of this book being as valuable and detailed as possible (and with my deep desire to help you to actually make progress with your book), I want to be sure we cover all bases.

The premise of this audit is to really take an objective look at how we can analyse some of the different ideas you might have and, subsequently, figure out how these can be transformed into a lead-generating non-fiction book. In mind of this, the audit centres on establishing the areas in which you have the most experience and then detailing the resources and degree of passion and enthusiasm you have for that area. This allows you to 'score' each book idea. The concept with the most points is clearly the most ideal to start with.

This strategy has also proven to be incredibly helpful when prospective clients communicate their desire to write a book before then following up with, 'But I just don't know what I'd even write a book about…' I'm a firm believer that everyone—every single soul on this planet—has at least one book inside of them (which is something I teach day-to-day in my business), and I'm also a huge believer that once you have come to know and to learn the strategies and techniques needed to write good books (and once you've seen how quick, easy and, dare I say, *enjoyable* the whole book-planning, -writing, and -publication process can be), you'll believe you have many, many, many books inside of you. Honestly, the possibilities are endless (as you're about to see for yourself), and as this becomes more and more apparent, you'll start to feel a spark of excitement ignite inside of you that reaffirms, yes, you can write many books, if you choose to do so.

This will be the first of many books, I'm sure.

—CARRIE RYAN
Mastermind Client

I'm honestly so excited to see how this activity unfolds for you, as I know it's an amazing way to get inspired and feel reassured that what you bring to the table can really, really help somebody who needs your knowledge and your experience.

THE EXPERIENCE = BOOKS AUDIT

There are five steps to this strategy, which should take no more than twenty minutes for you to complete. I would urge you to get involved: complete this audit and actually progress through all stages, even if you do know exactly what direction you want to go in, as you'll find it so valuable and inspiring when it comes to potentially incorporating more books into your future writing plans.

(Side Note: I have taken the liberty of creating a downloadable worksheet for you (see Resources), which you can either print out and complete by hand or fill in digitally. You're welcome!)

STEP 1: PAIN POINTS/EXPERIENCE

The first step focuses on your areas of experience.

When you open the worksheet linked above, you'll see there is a 'Pain Point/Experience' section. In this section, make a list of every single area you have experience in. Brain-dump them—that is, don't engage the analytical brain that tells you not to include something. If you have doubt, include it anyway. There will be so many, and this is a good thing. Don't stop until you can't think of any more to add. Your list might include areas like getting a young child to sleep through the night, or overcoming trauma, or setting up a business. All of these are pain points that other people are currently experiencing and want to move through, and they're all areas you were once completely inexperienced in, so imagine how many people could benefit from what you have to share.

Think about that exhausted new mother; how she feels and how desperately she wants to find a way to settle her young baby and get her to sleep through the night.

Imagine how many people have been affected by some kind of trauma and need to appease or overcome that.

Or the amount of people looking to launch and scale a business just as you have done, but really don't know the first thing about getting started.

As a common thread in my mentorship programs, I regularly highlight the importance of this activity and quite how needle-moving it can be, not only with reaffirming how qualified you are to write a book, but also with getting those creative juices flowing. To see a list like this come together—

to go from a blank worksheet to one overflowing with ideas—is so validating.

I believe anyone can easily come up with at least fifty or so different areas of experience. I would advise brainstorming at least ten different pain points that you have navigated yourself, whether in your professional or personal life, and write them down. Remember, if you have progressed through something and come out the other end, you're at least one step (if not many steps) ahead of someone who hasn't even started yet, and that's what matters here.

STEP 2: NICHE

The second step (and next column in the worksheet) pertains to niche. This is (arguably) self-explanatory: it is where you'll note down the specific niche your book would fall into.

As examples:

You might have learned how to use baby-safe essential oils or nature sounds or baby massage to achieve a full night's sleep for you and baby. In this case, your book would fall into the 'parenting' niche.

Maybe you've devised a new method or process to help your Ideal Clients manage their trauma and alleviate its day-to-day effects. You would categorise this as 'self-help'.

Or you might have successfully launched your own business, or scaled someone else's business, until it generated $1 million a year. In these cases, the niche would be 'business'.

STEP 3: RESOURCES

Next, we move onto resources. Here, you'll rank on a scale of one to ten how many resources you think you have available to you in each area.

For the sake of this activity, 'resources' may be defined as your direct experience, your training, the people you have available on your team, any contacts or acquaintances who can give you additional value or insights, or even research tools, such as Google and books. How much knowledge do you have at your fingertips, in your mind, or otherwise readily available?

If you know the niche to which your idea pertains inside out and you're able to speak on the subject for hours on end, or you could easily brain-dump everything you know really quickly (in other words, if you're an absolute boss in this area), assign a score of ten and pop it in the 'Resources' column on your worksheet.

STEP 4: ENTHUSIASM

As the fourth step (again, most likely self-explanatory), we consider how much this area excites you. Ask yourself:

How motivated am I to share my knowledge with other people to get them doing what I've done and achieving the results that I have achieved?

How excited am I to imagine taking someone trapped in a 9–5 and giving them the building blocks to them living life independently as the owner of their own business?

How passionate am I about helping coaches stuck in feast-or-famine to a point of consistent monthly earnings?

How happy would it make me to give someone the tools to launch and scale their very own million-dollar publishing house?

Again, this column requires a score of one to ten, where ten represents total excitement, alignment, and eagerness to get started.

STEP 5: SCORING

When you've completed the worksheet and you feel like you couldn't possibly have any more 'Pain Point/Experience' areas to brain-dump (though I warn you, more and more will start dropping in over the coming hours and days, so you'll probably want to keep your worksheet to hand for more book ideas!), take a look at your list. Be warned: this tends to provide a really, really powerful lightbulb moment for people!

Every item in the 'Experience' column is a book waiting to be written. In other words, every single item could potentially be a book that *you* could write.

As an example, one of my own Pain Point/Experience inclusions might be creating a program taking people through the book-writing process. Because I've done that—because I've navigated that entire process and walked my clients through to success—I could write a book on that. And *voila!* Here it is!

I am also more than qualified to teach people on the pain points, the solutions, the best processes, and the results they can achieve when it comes to the publication process as a whole.

Not to mention ghostwriting.

And launching an award-winning publishing company.

And scaling a business to seven figures.

Just allow that to simmer and process for a moment; you have in front of you one powerful list!

Next, it's time to add up the scores:

Take a look at the score you have assigned to the Resources and your Enthusiasm columns for each of your respective book ideas, and see which of them ranks the highest.

The highest-ranking concept is the one you feel most knowledgeable and experienced in, and most excited about. Common sense would suggest this being the right book for you to start tackling first, because this is the one that you feel the most capable of writing.

If you need reassurance in that regard, just take a look at your Resources column. As evidenced on your list, this is the book you feel most capable of writing and the one that you feel the most excited about. When you're progressing through the planning and writing processes, you'll want to feel capable and motivated, which will allow writing to come together easily and quickly. If ever you question or doubt, the Resources and Enthusiasm columns will gently remind you you're on the right track.

This stage in the process, while really simple, is so important. Quite honestly, it ignites in my clients excitement and feelings of competence and proficiency—not only for their main profession, but in so many different areas. It allows them to truly step into and embrace (and even *remember*) quite how easily they can rise to the challenge.

This system provides a solid way of showing you which publication you not necessarily *should* work on first, but which it makes the most sense to work on first, in mind of efficiency and enjoyability.

With that said, if (as mentioned at the beginning of this chapter) you've already chosen and committed to a particular book idea, that's absolutely fine. This activity is there to reassure and inspire you that not only are you more than capable of writing one book, but that you can actually write and publish many.

You can keep on implementing the techniques I share with you, whether here in this book or inside my programs, now and into the future. You can write and produce book after book after book without feeling limited and without questioning whether you bring enough to the table.

To reaffirm why you should write your book, you've ascertained that you are more than equipped to take someone experiencing a particular pain point and, through your own experience, lead them forward and further away from their current situation.

That is, without question, something worth sharing.

ACTION STEPS: CHAPTER 5

1. Move through the Experience = Books Audit, available at: www.entrepreneurbooksuccess.com/audit.
   By going through this process, you're affirming to yourself that not only do you have the tools and passion to justify you writing this book, but that you could actually continue your journey as an author with a multitude of different books in your future.

2. Share inside the Facebook group whether you found this strategy valuable, what book you're committed to writing, and your key takeaways for Chapter 5:
   www.facebook.com/groups/entrepreneurbooksuccess.

3. Declare to your social media following that you're going to write a book on your chosen concept. This will not only hold you accountable, but it will also inspire you to see this through. As soon as you have people commenting, asking questions, and showing appreciation for your book (which isn't even written yet!), you'll come to fully appreciate how much your book is already needed and wanted.

4. Tag me in your social media post (on Facebook, Instagram, or LinkedIn), and I'll be sure to shower your post with love. Use the hashtag #EntrepreneurBookSuccess so that I don't miss it.

CHECKLIST: CHAPTER 5

1. Completed the Experience = Books Audit.
2. Shared your progress, wins, thoughts, and breakthroughs inside the Facebook group.
3. Posted on social media.
4. Tagged me and used the book hashtag: #EntrepreneurBookSuccess.

CHAPTER 6
A TRANSFORMATIONAL JOURNEY

DON'T SAVE YOUR BEST FOR WHEN YOU THINK THE
MATERIAL CALLS FOR IT. ALWAYS BRING YOUR FULL
POTENTIAL.

—GABRIELLE UNION
Actress and Producer

THE READER'S A–Z TRANSFORMATIONAL JOURNEY is, without question, the most critical component of any lead-generating book. It is the foundational piece that facilitates, underpins, and is responsible for everything else that happens between you and your reader going forward: whether they come to know, like, and trust you; whether they will want to work with you way beyond the pages of the book; whether they will believe that you truly are the expert they need to help them going forward.

Whatever your book-related goals may be, they all hang on this transformational journey.

In a nutshell, it's not something to be overlooked.

WHAT IS THE READER'S A–Z TRANSFORMATIONAL JOURNEY?

The concept of the Reader's A–Z Transformational Journey is something I first devised when I created my book-planning and -writing course, The Non-Fiction Success Blueprinting Program™, in 2005. Essentially, the premise centres on moving your reader from one point to another, with a significant, high-value transformation experienced along the way.

When you're mapping out your book, your reader's journey should always be the very first step in this process. In actual fact, it should be your focal point whenever you progress your book in any way, but particularly during the blueprinting/outlining process. It should be your laser focus. It should be your guiding star and compass whenever you come to add any single piece of content. Concentrating on your reader and their progression should always be at the forefront of your mind:

Does my reader need this?

Will my reader benefit from this?

What does my reader need in order to progress at this point?

By focusing on your reader and how you can provide them with a transformation, the very core of your book will be centred on value and moving your reader to where you need them to be so that they can move into an 'off the page' relationship with you and be an absolute dream to work with. By doing this, you'll see a very clear path your reader needs to follow.

As an example, when first deciding to work with me on her book, my client Jessa knew she wanted to take her readers from the pain point of dreaming of starting their own digital products business but not knowing how, all the way through to them setting up their business and creating a few preliminary products. At this point (by the end of her book), they would then be qualified enough to enrol into a low-ticket monthly membership focused on scaling their business, building up their product inventory, and achieving consistent sales.

At the very beginning of our work together, Jessa knew she did not want to grow her business with her book in a way that would make more work for her, such as by encouraging people to work with her 1:1. Rather, her goals for the book were to grow her social media presence, monthly memberships, and group coaching.

By being very intentional about her goals in combination with what the process needed to look like for her clients, she was able to formulate an avatar of her 'ideal reader' and have absolute clarity about their transformational journey. This allowed her to remain very conscious throughout the planning and writing process about what needed to be covered and how she would lead her readers from Point A to Point Z.

Not to mention what needed to be covered in between.

As an expert in your field, the 'in between' points of the A–Z will no doubt come very naturally, but asking questions on behalf of your reader will make things so much easier:

What do they need in order to progress from Point A to Point Z?

What do they need to know?

What do they need to have learned?

What changes do they need to have implemented?

What behaviours do they need to have adopted?

What do they need to believe?

When we get clear on what the journey needs to look like (in all of its specifics), so much falls into place, and the transformation happens very quickly, naturally, and powerfully.

WHY IS ALL OF THIS SO IMPORTANT?

Why is the Reader's A–Z Transformational Journey so important? Because your book is not about you; it's about your reader.

This is a point I labour over and over again inside our publishing house, whether when taking clients through the book-planning process, when completing ghostwriting interviews, or when undertaking cover design during the publication process:

Your book is not about you. It's about your readers.

This is one of my most commonly repeated lessons inside our mastermind.

If you can train your mind to constantly remember this—to keep it looping any time you do anything to do with your book, whether planning, writing, or marketing—you'll find that your book will be an altogether more valuable, more transformational read. And your audience will thank you for it.

It's not about you. It's about your readers.

For CEOs, entrepreneurs, coaches, and all-round professionals, the transformational journey you take your reader on isn't too complex a concept: if your business is already successful and your offer has been validated, leading people on a journey is something you've already learned how to do—and do well.

Your Reader's Transformational Journey is not too different to the client transformations you create in your business: it's all about moving your readers—your dreamy prospects—from where they are at present to closer to where they need to be.

It's not about you. It's about your readers.

However, it's critical to note that this isn't to say you should solve the problem in its entirety. In actuality, you need to be absolutely sure you *don't* do that, or your readers-turned-ready-to-buy-prospects couldn't possibly benefit from your services in the future. But it *is* to say that you want to change the reality of where your reader is, how they feel, and how they view *you* as the expert positioned to help them.

It's not about you. It's about your readers.

It could be that you provide a handful of valuable strategies they can implement in their business to allow them to move from a haphazard social media presence to a more engaging, more consistent feed.

It could be that you show them how to neutralise difficult situations or communicate better with their spouse.

It could be that you outline exactly how they can get started on the project of a lifetime—like writing and publishing a book or building their own publishing company!—so that they no longer feel lost or like their goal is unattainable.

Whatever your industry and whatever your niche, the emphasis is on continuously questioning where your client is in their journey and what you can share throughout the book to move them away from their pain point and closer to resolution.

It's not about you. It's about your readers.

Do this well, and you will position yourself as a trusted authority and expert with the skillset to do what you say you can do. Your readers will then emerge from your book feeling inspired, motivated, encouraged, and capable, and like you are the right expert to help them with the next stage of their journey.

It's not about you. It's about your readers.

WHERE TO BEGIN: POINT A

The first step in your Reader's A–Z Transformational Journey is to get to know everything you possibly can about your ideal reader (your Dream Client) and where they're at when they pick up your book. You can base this on the most amazing clients you've worked with.

This first point in the transformational journey should come very easily, as it isn't too dissimilar to profiling your Ideal Client avatar for your business, which you more than likely have done on a number of occasions already and for every offer and solution you've created. It's all about considering what their goals and ideals are. What would they love to see happen? What results would be business- and/or life-changing for them? What would absolutely blow them away? And what struggles are they experiencing in getting those results?

It's important to be mindful of not only their pain point (which you are trying to move them away from), but also their dreamiest of scenarios (even if they don't fully articulate what exactly that dream scenario would be). As examples, in the past, it was super-common for me to hear different fear-based objections from my target audience:

I don't have the time to write a book.

It just isn't a priority right now.

My business isn't ready for a book.

I'm not qualified enough to write a book.

I've heard it's hard to make books successful.

And then, in the same breath, they would communicate quite how badly they wanted, imagined, and dreamed of having the results:

I've always wanted to be a published author.

I can't even imagine how amazing it would feel to hold my book in my hands.

International Bestseller... You can help with that?
The book doing the selling for me... That would be so amazing.
Leads paying to become leads... Wow.

I knew very early on that so many of my then-ideal audience's objections were fear-based, and I also knew that that particular client base wasn't fully expressing how incredible they would feel if any of the above dream scenarios were to come to fruition—again, because they were scared to hope for even some of them. But fast-forward to when I began profiling my absolute Dream Clients, and those 'objections' and results ended up changing. That is, the objections stopped being objections and instead became genuine points of struggle:

I am so ready to write this book, but I just don't know where to start.

I am so ready to invest the time, but I need to know how much.

I am so ready to publish a book I can be proud of, but I don't know the first thing about publishing.

I am so ready to expand my reach, but I don't know how to make the book globally available.

I am so ready to uplevel, but I don't know how to market myself to Bestseller.

And the dream results also significantly changed:

I'd love if this book could genuinely impact someone. Even if it's just one person, I would love that.

It would be amazing if this book could generate income for the business, but I also just want to help people.

I would love to become a published author. I'd love to prove to myself I can do this.

And perhaps one of the most amazing things is that my Dream Clients absolutely know the areas in which they are skilled and what their zone of genius is (and what it isn't), meaning they know and understand the power and benefits to finding the right expert to help them and trusting in the process.

The truly amazing thing about all of this is that by honing in on your absolute Dream Client and speaking to them from the very beginning of the book (from Point A in their transformational journey), you're not only helping them, but also yourself: you're inviting into your space only those who fit the Dream Client profile and speaking exclusively to them and helping them with where they are—which is very different to where the non-Ideal Clients stand.

And then imagine quite how blown away your clients end up being when you flood their world with benefits they didn't ever imagine, or at least weren't fixated on.

I experienced this in 2022 when delivering a free hour-long training inside a Facebook group. One of the attendees, who later turned out to be Scyller Borglum (the Vice President of WSP USA), was watching attentively and taking pages of notes. After the training ended, she then added me as a contact, subscribed to our email list, and scheduled a call for the next day (note the fast action and serious implementation). On our call, Scyller told me how she had already written the first draft of her manuscript and had just been patiently waiting to find the right person to publish it. She shared with me how despite it being early morning and her being on a late flight the night before, and despite being in an airport hotel, she couldn't miss the opportunity to speak with me. She showed up, fully committed, and trusted in me to guide her. Scyller recognised (even with five degrees to her name and as an absolute powerhouse in her field) that there was huge value to be found in finding the right experts for what she wanted to achieve: professional publication.

> I definitely need your help. I need the professional edits and the cover design, and I'd love to achieve International Bestseller. I'm happy to go out and promote and talk to different groups and do social media lives, but I need your help!
>
> I need someone who has access to the publishing world, someone who can make everything beautiful, and I just don't have the bandwidth to figure all of that out myself. So, what are the next steps?
>
> —SCYLLER BORGLUM
> *Vice President of WSP USA*

A short time later, after signing with us to complete her publication, she reiterated her thoughts and approach to the process when sending me an excerpt from a book she was reading. It said:

A professional recognises her limitations.

She gets an agent, she gets a lawyer, she gets an accountant. She knows she can only be a professional at one thing. She brings in other pros and treats them with respect.

—STEVEN PRESSFIELD
Author of The War of Art

That completely sums up not only how Scyller showed up in our business as a complete Dream Client, but also how your book can absolutely attract your own versions of Scyller.

Meet your client where they are at (at their Point A) and use the language that resonates with them as you discuss leading them to their ideal end result, and they will know, with certainty, that they are in safe hands.

This first step in your readers' journey will allow you to call in those clients who prioritise what you prioritise and what your business and mission truly count for and represent at their core, and then you'll be free to underpromise and overdeliver.

My own clients witness this every single day. Those clients who stress how thrilled they'd be if their book were to touch just one person end up absolutely blown away when they see thousands of people adding their book to their TBR list on Goodreads™.

They end up speechless when they find their book at #1 on Amazon in the U.S.A, U.K., Canada, Australia, and more.

They're delighted every single time a new opportunity presents itself, or they receive a new follower on social media, or a new client reaches out to secure their services—all after reading their book.

It never gets old.

So, although Point A on this journey will, to some extent, feel like something you've navigated time and time before, my advice to you when formulating your *reader*'s starting point would be to take the example of where your dreamiest of clients was at when they initially came to you, and use that as the foundation for this initial step. Your book and the entire journey you'll lead your reader on is a golden opportunity to be super-intentional about who you want in your world and how they show up, so squeeze every bit of goodness out of that.

WHERE TO END: POINT Z

One question I am commonly asked focuses on word count and the length of the book.

Is 50,000 words enough?

How long should a book be?

How many pages should my book be?

I want my book to be *x* number of pages or *x* number of words. How do I make that happen?

I can completely understand why word or page count feels like a valuable guide point. Writers discuss these parameters often, and any Internet search on helpful guidelines will often yield results with some very specific ranges. However, it's important to note a couple of things:

1. First, the more rigid word count recommendations commonly relate to fiction, such as young adult, fantasy, and sci-fi, rather than non-fiction. Even still, upon examining horror, as an example, with its recommended range of 40,000–80,000 words, it's evident upon reviewing the works of the most successful horror author of all time, Stephen King, that any perceived rigidity actually counts for nothing: *Carrie* totals a little over a modest 61,000 words, while *It* exceeds a monstrous 445,000 words.

    Even if we look specifically at different non-fiction genres and the suggested word count ranges, the scale spans so far and wide that there really is very little point in there being any degree of guide in the first place. Take self-help books, for example (business, marketing, routine, habits, 'how-to', and so on): the recommended range is stated by some in the field as being anything from 30,000–70,000 words. That's a huge difference between the lower and higher end of the scale. Memoir, on the other hand, is suggested as being most optimal at anything in the 40,000–80,000 words range. Again, the two differ wildly.

    With these ranges and guidelines so loose, I can't help but wonder why so much emphasis has been placed on staying within them, when authors across the globe are simply writing until there is nothing else left to say—and getting successful from doing it.

2. The second point to note is that the publishing industry is changing quickly, and although it still remains rooted in a number

of different, old-fashioned ideals, advances in technology have meant more and more independent writers and publishers are committing fully to sending out into the world whatever resonates with them and whatever their specific market asks for. They are becoming less and less concerned with cementing the *amount* of content they feel qualified to share or with boxing themselves into a corner with the strict instructions that they 'mustn't move until they've penned 90,000 words'. They know that approach simply doesn't work, so they just write until they're done writing.

As someone who is not only the CEO of a publishing house but also a writer of eighteen years, I am a firm believer in writing until the story is complete. That's it. I believe in the reader being taken on a journey and that journey lasting however long it needs to last, regardless of genre. To pad out a book or fill it with fluff for no reason other than to bump up the word count so as to meet old and outdated prerequisites really does not resonate with me—and it won't resonate with your reader. All that really does it waste your reader's time and degrade the overall quality of your work. Not to mention the fact that authority-stamping non-fiction books like this one (and the book *you* will write!) are aimed at fast-acting, self-led, forward-thinking entrepreneurs and professionals who want to develop themselves and be productive and proactive. That means they tend to prioritise getting to the gold as quickly as possible without wasting their time on filler.

In short, there are countless *should*s shouted at us across pretty much all areas of life, and book-writing is no different. However, writing and publishing a book (while albeit a strategic undertaking in the case of your lead-generating book) remains a creative endeavour, and that means you can absolutely justify doing things your way without boxing yourself in.

It's also really important to recognise that while one person might praise and recommend a particular 100,000-word self-help book, another might just as highly recommend the quick airplane read that was all but 20,000 words. In my time spent dedicated to this industry, I have witnessed no real correlation between word count and average reader enjoyment or engagement.

In conclusion, whenever a client poses any iteration of this question or probes for guidelines pertaining to this issue, my answer is always the same: you know your book is finished when you can look at your reader's journey and know, with absolute certainty, that you have provided a transformation. It doesn't matter if your book is 40,000 words long or 140,000 words long. The most important thing is that you've managed to help your reader make a shift, witness change, and learn something new. Succeed in moving them further away from their pain point and closer to achieving the result of their dreams, and your book is done.

As per the classic children's book, *Alice's Adventures in Wonderland*, written by Lewis Carroll:

> *'Begin at the beginning,' the King said gravely, 'and go on till you come to the end: then stop.'*

Although not a fairytale story, your book is no different. A high-value needle-moving non-fiction is all about providing value and making it easy for your audience to succeed. Don't forget: it's not about you, it's about your readers. If you allow *that* to be your focus, you really can't go wrong, word count be damned.

THE IN BETWEEN: MARKERS

When you're clear on exactly who your dream reader is, where they are (Point A), and where they need to end up by the end of your book (Point Z), the 'in between' comes together so much easier. You need to know your destination before you start driving. When we have those two points (where we are starting and where our destination is) locked in before we set off, the journey is so much easier to formulate.

Inside my programs about blueprinting and mapping out your book, the points between A and Z are referred to as 'markers'. In short, these markers present the different milestones your reader needs to pass through in order to progress from where they are to where you want them to be, cover to cover. When moving your reader across all the stages necessary to facilitate transformation, each of these markers will allow for significant developments and will ultimately form each of your book's chapters.

Allow me to repeat: your markers become your book's chapters.

(In mind of helping you to truly visualise how this works, I have created a free mini training for you inside of my academy, which expands on this point with my Flip = Contents approach.)

This stage of the blueprinting process requires that you take a look at every single stage you would ordinarily lead your clients through when taking them from pain point to resolution. At this stage, don't worry about giving away too much gold or oversharing on the juiciness; clarity as to what to share and when will come in the next chapter (Chapter 7). For now, consider how client results are achieved in the daily running of your business.

Take this book as an example:

During the past seventeen years, when it comes to taking my Dream Clients from their Point A (being ready to write and publish a book, but just not knowing where to begin, how much time it's going to take, or what a book can truly offer, both personally and professionally) through to their Point Z (knowing how to become the author of a professionally published, globally available, International Bestselling book that attracts and nurtures warm leads from book to business), I have come to identify my clients' needing to progress through three different phases:

First, understanding the mechanics of a book. They need to be completely sold on the idea of a book: what a 'lead-generating book' actually is, what it can do for their business, how a book can take a business from unknown to fully booked, and the financial investment and returns. Accordingly, these different pieces form the initial leg of my reader's journey, or Part I of my book, because being completely sold on why an entrepreneur needs a book and how can they benefit will provide all the motivation and inspiration they could possibly need to not only begin, but to see the project through to the very end. *Without* this part of the journey, with its different mindset and strategic trainings, it would be far too easy for my readers to shrug and walk away, dismissing a book as a proficient way of growing and widening their business reach and impact entirely. *With* this part of the journey, however, my dream readers and future Dream Clients recognise a book as being a complete no-brainer of a move, and they are motivated to act accordingly.

The second phase is teaching them how to actually make progress with their book. This means taking them by the hand and leading them through actually starting the planning and writing process, including what it means to take their readers on a journey, and providing clear strategies on what needs to be included (and, just as importantly, what shouldn't be included), how and why unique lead magnets should be sprinkled in throughout the book, and how they'll know when their first draft is ready to turn over to their publisher or chosen editor. All these individual components are common pain points and the focus of frequently asked questions for my clients, so it makes sense for the journey I take my readers on to pass through all these key milestones. By creating this leg of the journey (which forms Part II of the book and provides their second phase of transformation), my readers will again progress and develop, learn strategies, and remove the most common stumbling blocks, such as where to begin and what to share.

The third phase is all about achieving success—notably through professional publication, ensuring a good pre-order period, trust and status stamps (e.g. International Bestseller), turning a book into a lead-generating machine, and whether or not ghostwriting might be a more feasible option in mind of the time investment—with all of this making up the final transformational phase (Part III).

My own work inside my business (which has spanned thousands of clients) has shown me, through many examples, how the dreamiest of prospective clients show up in my world and how they need to be led in order to achieve success. It is these client experiences—what they tell me they need, the problems they have experienced prior to working with me, and the concerns and doubts they have as they navigate the process—that have allowed me to formulate the most valuable, client-focused transformational journey; hence, the individual markers that make up this book's chapters.

It is this very same consideration and analysis that will allow you to formulate the most valuable, logical journey for your own readers and to devise the very best sequence for each of the milestones that become your markers/chapters.

To help you with formulating this journey, ask yourself these questions:

1. How do my clients usually feel when they initially enter my orbit?
2. What are some of the common thoughts communicated by my clients?
3. What would my clients' dreamy scenario be as far as results are concerned?
4. Do my clients fully know and understand the benefits they're going to reap through our work together?

5. Do my clients know what the process involves?
6. Are my clients aware of their own obligations and responsibilities when it comes to achieving results, and what my role as the professional involves?
7. What do my clients need to implement, and how do they need to show up in order for them to be successful?
8. What are the key stages my clients need to progress through?
9. What are the main things my clients need to learn to move forward?
10. What do my clients need to do in order to experience a good degree of success?
11. Are there varying degrees of success?
12. How would working with me in a closer capacity enhance my clients' results?

Of course, this is not an exhaustive list, but the point here is to always put yourself in your reader's/prospective client's shoes and consider what they need from you across all pages of your book. How can you offer value? How can you move them from Point A through to Point Z, and what does that process look like?

Continuously revert back to the reminder that your book is about your reader and the transformational journey will quickly take shape, because if you know your clients well and you believe fully, at a soul level, that your clients are able to achieve incredible results under your guidance (even just through what you will share in your book), you won't be able to help but create incredible, tangible results for them.

WHAT DOES A TRANSFORMATION LOOK LIKE?

Importantly, when I talk about the transformation your readers need to experience, I don't necessarily mean an absolutely mind-blowing, life-changing transformation by *your* standards. Remember: you're thick in your business and your own industry, so what you might consider to be highly transformational could actually prove to be too much and too soon for your reader. With this said, it's always far better for the transformation to be something small and manageable but nonetheless powerful.

Of course, the transformations you offer your clients inside of your business are always going to run deeper and be far more significant than what your book can possibly provide, but your book can still be pivotal in allowing your readers to develop key insights, new skills, and change the way they approach their goals.

It could be that by the end of your book, your readers have been able to implement the initial steps needed to launch a business, taking them from being stuck in a state of doing nothing more than dreaming to actually making progress and moving forward.

Maybe you have led them through successfully incorporating a new twenty-minute routine into their baby's sleep schedule, which now means their baby is sleeping better, with both parents better rested and on their way to self-settling a baby.

It could be that they have been able to add some simple ingredients into their diet to reduce cortisol levels as a part of their long-term journey to achieving health and fitness with you as their guide.

Whatever the transformation, small steps do not necessarily mean low-value or insignificant results. So, it's all about identifying what small, easily implemented, easily achievable wins you can offer to your reader so that they can see progress quickly, from cover to cover, and emerge not only feeling good about themselves, but experiencing results like they would never have expected from a book.

Again: it's all about your reader. Make them feel good, and they will associate you with that feeling and the huge wins they've had. With every stride they take, creeping closer and closer to their ultimate vision, they will trust in you more and more to lead them across the ultimate finish line.

As a case in point, when I very first started to work with one of my mastermind clients, she was experiencing some fear surrounding whether she could actually do this (write and publish a book); whether she was qualified to do this; whether it could be a success. Although she had grown to know and trust me, she still wondered whether *she* had what it would take to move through the process.

I directed her to a short video training I had done on fear—a twelve-minute video—and this proved to be so incredibly transformational for her that she then didn't so much as miss a beat in getting started. She threw herself in without reservation and never looked back.

She told me the next morning about how this video training had been life-changing for her; how she had felt a complete shift; how she now felt that she could write not just one book, but many more after it:

> *I feel like the earth moved a little. I had a very real shift. Your training changed my life yesterday. I feel like I can do anything now. Anything.*

> —LISA A. SMITH
> *'Retire by 45' Expert and Mentor*

From my perspective, I had no idea this mini training could ever prove to be quite so valuable, never mind 'life-changing', to my clients. Of course, I knew and recognised fear as being a key component in stopping my prospective clients from taking the step to begin working on a book—with this fear commonly masked with time- and financial-based excuses—but I hadn't realised it was quite so hindering for clients who had already initiated the journey.

With this new information came the opportunity to provide a pivotal transformation that could allow my clients to move forward. And it is this that's the key.

MICRO PROBLEMS

When the individual markers/chapters guiding your reader's journey have been outlined and you've 'locked in' the transformation your reader is going to experience, it's super-common to find yourself living out two very different moments:

Moment 1: *Oh, wow. This is amazing. My readers are going to love, love, love this! Here I was, wondering what I was going to share and how the book was going to develop, and here it is: A–Z. Clear as day. This transformation is insane. They're going to be blown away and absolutely jump at the chance of working with me!*

Moment 2: *Hang on a second... If I share all of this, there'll be no need for them to work with me! I've given it all away; all of the gold! How am I going to do this? How can I give readers of my book everything I've been* *teaching my 1:1 $50,000 clients? I can't possibly do that! This is a complete disaster!*

Both of these moments are completely normal and come up for pretty much every single client who is writing a book on their business transformations.

So, how do we handle this? Well, panic over, because it's really quite simple: we focus on teaching the *what* and the *why*, while sharing only very intentional pieces of the *how*, just as you might do when delivering a workshop or presentation, writing an article, or filming a mini training.

And herein lies the magic.

Before we delve into that, however, it's absolutely critical that you don't take steps back and rethink all the markers you've outlined and the journey you've mapped out thus far. It's essential you take your reader on the transformational journey you recognise they need and you know they want when they pick up your book, even if you understand that a) they don't yet fully know what they need and b) they *think* they know what they need.

In other words, allow me to affirm for you: the transformational journey you've outlined is absolutely the right journey. It's the journey that instinctively came to you; the journey that 'downloaded', so to speak. It's the journey you've recognised as being not only needed but valuable, and the one you yourself detailed as being the right journey for your clients. It was the right journey way before you attended to your panic stations or spiralled into a place of 'lack' with questions about whether your services will even be needed long after your reader has finished the book—and it continues to be the right journey now.

So, relax into what you've already determined to be the journey, and allow it to remain.

Now, back to the magic.

As we said before, the magic comes from teaching the *what* and the *why*, but only very select pieces of the *how*. The idea is that you identify which pieces of the *how* are absolute no-nos for sharing in your book—the ones your private clients potentially pay several thousand dollars (maybe more) for and that create the biggest results—and label these as strictly *what* and *why* elements. It's perfectly okay and reasonable for you to share how to achieve results, without sharing how to achieve the *biggest* results.

This isn't to say you won't be giving value, but it is to say you can create a transformation while reserving the huge, life-altering, goals-of-a-lifetime wins for those clients who truly move and act to work with you at closer proximity. Not to mention the fact that deep-diving into the many intricacies and details of everything you share with and do for your clients inside your business and its programs would more than likely expand way beyond a 'reasonably sized' book—and yes, I'm contradicting the whole word count discussion we just had, but I'm sure you would agree, when you really think about it.

So, how do we choose which areas should be the ones we sprinkle with magic?

Well, we dig deep into micro problems.

Inside my mastermind and self-guided program, I talk about micro problems often. In the context of books and engaging with your reader, these are the common obstacles your clients come up against and the key pieces they need to navigate in order to move away from their current pain point. What micro problems *aren't* are the pivotal cornerstones of your high-ticket programs.

I advise my mastermind and blueprinting clients to solve between three and five micro problems, as this provides significant value while allowing readers to learn, implement, make progress, see success, and note wins. This approach also positions you as the expert without compromising your trusted processes or giving away too much intellectual property. Identify the micro problems that will give the most valuable, transformation-inducing results by thinking about your clients (Dream Clients only) and considering: what have they found to be truly needle-moving? Don't disregard the answers that come to mind even if you wouldn't necessarily highlight a particular area as being a core part of your process; these are the teachings your readers will think of as the most valuable, even if you don't share the same feeling.

For me, I've had clients talk about how they used to worry about their book being lost in the noise as a result of supposed market saturation—until I led them through the huge growth of the book industry, coupled with its projected worth of U.S. $164 billion by 2030.

I've also had clients voice their worries about the time it would take to write a book and whether they have the bandwidth to do so (these people have become lost in the narrative that books take years to write) before then learning they can fully blueprint and write their book in four to six months by committing just seventeen minutes a day.

Another huge needle-mover is quite how many ways there are to monetise a book and how the revenue comes from sales *from* the book and not sales *of* the book—again, a pivotal transformation in the way books are viewed and the all-too-common misconception that royalties are the key performance indicator (note: royalties couldn't be more inconsequential).

All these huge shifts, as voiced by not just one but many of my clients, can't be even closely considered 'key pieces' in my teachings or core lessons in my mastermind curriculum. Nonetheless, my clients have taken huge leaps forward when guided on these points, simply because the 'brain noise' that comes with these areas has previously hindered (if not altogether stopped) their progress.

I would be very surprised if your own clients don't have similar action-preventing blocks.

THE RESULTS

Getting inside the heart, mind, and soul of your Dream Client is fundamental to the book-writing process. To lean in and listen to what your most Ideal Clients have expressed they want (while identifying, as the professional you are, exactly what they need) is incredibly powerful if you are to take potentially cold readers and shape them into beautifully warm leads who know, like, and trust you and who want to soak up everything you have to share.

As has been reiterated throughout this chapter, your book is not about you, but your readers, and if you can form the backbone of your book to echo this forever-looping premise, your readers will emerge lightyears away from where they began—and that's truly what this is all about.

Your book is a lead-generating tool, yes. It can attract dreamy readers and direct them into your business as high-ticket-paying clients, absolutely. It can make superfans out of once-cold followers, with certainty. But your book also has the potential to be the very first steppingstone your ideal audience takes in pursuing their goal, whatever that may be, and they're trusting you to guide them through them taking that first leap (reading your book).

The importance of taking your reader on a value-centred, transformational journey is not a lesson I have wanted to merely gloss over in this book; it's paramount and all-important. I would actually argue it's the singular most important component of a lead-generating book: even if you were to fail to incorporate any call-to-actions or after-the-book directions, those readers who have grown to know, like, and trust you and who are adamant they want you to guide them on the rest of their journey will absolutely seek you out (though make no mistake: giving them the CTAs makes things infinitely easier). On the other hand, if you focus only on the sale (sell, sell sell!) without truly, deeply caring about moving your reader forward, your book will fulfil very little of its potential.

AS AN ADDED BONUS...

What I really love about my blueprinting system (and not just what I've taught here in this section of the book, but across the full program) is that it's common for my clients to reap a number of unexpected benefits as a result of what they learn:

> It made me think about the way I teach in a completely different way, and so I started using it to plan out my YouTube™ videos. That has been a revelation. That process is responsible for my biggest ever YouTube™ video—it's my best performing—and it was picked up by one of the biggest software companies in my niche. They actually now feature the video inside their software.

> —JESSA BELLMAN
> *Digital Products Coach*

And then:

> I use your blueprinting system when I'm planning out my program videos for inside my program. It's really helped me to think about where my clients are at and what I need to cover in every video.

> —LISA A. SMITH
> *'Retire by 45' Expert & Mentor*

To conclude: if you can solve a problem (or many problems) commonly experienced by your ideal target audience, you will very naturally be positioned as a trustworthy authority in their mind. Move them further away from their pain point by solving three to five micro problems, and your readers will be not only mildly curious about how to work with you further, but proactive in investing their time and/or money into whatever else is waiting for them behind the curtain.

ACTION STEPS: CHAPTER 6

1. Profile your Dreamy Clients.
2. Begin to outline your Reader's Transformational Journey:
   - Point A: Where are they in their journey when they pick up your book?
   - Point Z: Where do you want them to be when they have finished reading?
3. Brainstorm and solidify the transformation you want your reader to have experienced so they are the perfect match for working with you.
   - Look at the milestones your reader needs to progress through to go from Point A to transformation.
4. Identify micro problems:
   - Scour your testimonials, read through past emails, revisit DMs, and relisten to voice notes.
   - Sit down and carefully identify all the common threads and wins your clients share that you wouldn't necessarily categorise as being at the core of your signature offerings. Finalise three to five micro problems for providing value and moving your reader further away from their pain point.
5. Share your key takeaways for Chapter 6 inside our Facebook group at www.facebook.com/groups/entrepreneurbooksuccess.

CHECKLIST: CHAPTER 6

1. Completed your 'Dreamy Client' profile.
2. Outlined the preliminary steps of your Reader's Transformational Journey.

3. Brainstormed and made progress with your Reader's Transformational Journey.
4. Determined your three to five micro problems for solving.
5. Shared your key takeaways for Chapter 6 inside our Facebook group.

CHAPTER 7
WHAT TO INCLUDE (AND WHAT *NOT* TO INCLUDE)

WHAT YOU GET BY ACHIEVING YOUR GOALS IS NOT AS
IMPORTANT AS WHAT YOU BECOME BY ACHIEVING YOUR
GOALS.

—ZIG ZIGLAR (1926–2012)
Bestselling Author and Speaker

W HEN RUNNING A PUBLISHING HOUSE specialising in works of a lead-generating, authoritative nature, the issue of what content one should include in their book (and, just as importantly, what they really *shouldn't* include) arises regularly. Should this be included, or not?

It's difficult to provide a one-size-fits-all answer to this, as everyone's business (and, therefore, book) is different. However, there are still some principles that, if permitted to guide (though not dictate) you, can help you to write a book that is beautifully balanced in terms of providing value and moving your reader forward, and ensuring you don't give away too much. After all, you don't want to give away so much that your readers have need no further help from you. That would be the absolute worst-case scenario: that your book overdelivers so much so that your services are rendered surplus to requirements.

In addition to the balancing act that is 'giving value' versus 'not oversharing', it's also critical that several other components be included in your book, all of which have the role of developing know, like, and trust, and directing your reader to your business.

And then there are the optional pieces that make for a better, more comprehensive experience for your reader. You might choose to incorporate some or all of these, but I would always recommend the inclusion of as many as possible.

All of this will be discussed here in this chapter, with the various elements broken down into a sort of checklist. Read through this as you consider starting your book, and enjoy the realisation that little seedlings of ideas are bursting into life and bringing with them a flood of excitement. And, of course, don't forget to make a note of what those little seedlings are so that you can come back and tend to them. Lost ideas are the worst.

When you begin to blueprint your book, come back to this chapter and try to tick off as many of these inclusions as possible as you add them into your book. Trust me, the additional time and attention will prove so worth it, and will pay dividends over and over. Your reader will appreciate the countless little nuggets of gold, and will end up being so committed to your process that they will stay the course, achieve the results, and want to immerse themselves in your world way beyond the pages of your book.

WHAT TO INCLUDE

VALUE

Of course, this has already been noted, emphasised, and reiterated many times over in this book (and we're only 127 pages in), but the value you provide in your book cannot and should not be underestimated. It's what your readers are looking for:

Value in new strategies.

Value in new knowledge.

Value in new ways of thinking.

Value in removing glass ceilings.

Value in believing they can do this.

Value in being *shown* they can do this.

Value in knowing they can achieve more.

Value in being shown the steps to get there.

Value in making new, never-done-before progress.

Everything you do and share inside your book must really and truly push the envelope and allow your reader to shift, change, and move forward.

It needs to do all of it.

We only ever do things in order to receive value in some form or another. At first thought, you might reject that statement and want to stress how you do things every single day that 'don't benefit you', but I would argue the opposite to be true: whether an action allows you to achieve something or prevents a negative outcome or alleviates a struggle of some kind, everything is done in mind of the belief that the trade-off is worth it; that some good is going to come out of this action. It's with that in mind that you want to give as much value as you can to your reader. Your reader isn't reading your book to fill the time, without any hope of getting something out of it. As we've already discussed, your readers are more than likely forward-thinking, fast-moving professionals who want to learn and invest in their self-development, so be sure to give them what they need in order to achieve that goal. Waste their time and give them nothing but fluff, and nobody will be reaching out to thank you.

A RESOLUTION TO THREE TO FIVE MICRO PROBLEMS

Although already discussed in depth in the previous chapter, this remains one of the most important transformational components for inclusion in your book, so it's deserving of a revisit.

To reiterate, we want to be sure we move our readers further away from their current pain point (Point A) and closer to their dream scenario, without giving away all the gold. This is done by identifying the micro problems that your clients have commonly shared with you and the solutions of which have proven needle-moving and high-value for your clients, and sharing the *how* behind how your reader can solve these micro problems for themselves.

When you take a look at all of the micro problems you currently solve for your clients (potentially without even realising or thinking twice about it), you'll come to see, very clearly, how much value you have to share that can provide your readers with a complete transformation, without you oversharing. Look at these micro problems and establish which have proven to be the most valuable for your clients. The best way to do this is to ask them; you'll find they'll be more than happy and willing to share their progress. Then, detail the solutions to these micro problems in your book.

Again (and this cannot be emphasised enough), by focusing your efforts on solving these problems for your readers, you are not only providing immense value—key life- and business-changing shifts for only the cost of a book? What?!—but you're also showcasing your own expertise, your authority and status in your field, and your ability to walk the walk with leading your clients from pain to resolution.

It's a win–win for all.

AS MUCH OF THE WHAT *AND THE* WHY *AS POSSIBLE*

Even though it seems to go against the grain for most entrepreneurs to share only the *what* and the *why*, this is a key element in giving value without negating your reader's need to become a client.

When I was first upping my game in the entrepreneurial world (which involved me handing my editing business over to my eldest daughter and committing full steam ahead to our publishing house), my mentor at the time, Grace Lever, advised that in business, we should look to 'teach and leave a void'. She stressed the importance of this—of giving value, but still leaving enough room for your prospective client to take more steps, really commit to the process, and further their progress.

As business owners and thought leaders, we have a natural propensity and inclination to give as much as we can, because we're genuinely so invested in being able to wave a magic wand and solve our clients' problems. While this is not a bad way to be as a human being, it doesn't necessarily make for the most profitable lead-generating books.

I came to see this for myself when working on the book of one of my incredible clients, Murisa Harba, an award-winning actor and director and author of the International Bestseller *Acting with Energy*. Murisa, with her signature techniques that support actors in uplevelling their careers, was deeply invested in giving her readers quite literally everything she could pour out of herself and onto the page. She wanted them to benefit at every turn of the page, and was concerned, at her very core, with helping her audience to succeed. The result? A book that gave away quite literally all the gold. Honourable? Yes. Generous? Absolutely. But we knew that not only did Murisa and her company deserve to benefit from her book by leading readers to the gold offered in her programs and courses, but that her readers also needed to learn and implement without overwhelm—and we risked overwhelm if we were to go all in with too much too soon.

Quite honestly, Murisa's book and everything she shared was truly remarkable; our chief editor told me there was a book's worth of value in the opening chapter alone. That encapsulates who Murisa is as a person and business owner. Nevertheless, we sought to provide value by establishing a beautiful balance of the *what* and 'why' and then nuggets of the *how* that could move the reader forward, position Murisa as the authority she is, and leave her readers wanting more. The resulting publication did the job perfectly (testament to my team and all they do!).

It's important to emphasise that over the years, what I have come to learn is that sometimes, sharing the *what* and the *why* can be just as inspiring and induce just as much awe as you blueprinting the actual strategies in detail.

As an example, I recently did a free training on the time it takes for the average professional to plan, write, and publish their book to a good standard. As detailed in Chapter 14 (Ghostwriting), this can take as many as 150 hours. I then went on to discuss the fact that inside of my program, that time can drastically decrease to seventeen minutes a day, or two hours a week—a total of 100 hours. In short, when you have the right strategies and know exactly which steps to take (and when), you can save fifty hours (or a whopping 33%) of the time you would take if you were to go it alone.

Now, recognise here that I didn't share the *how* (i.e. the steps they'd have to take in order to save all this time). I shared the *what* (the fact it takes seventeen minutes a day) and the *why*.

The response from my audience was amazing. Christina Rowe, founder of the Stand Out! Media Group and owner of the huge 750,000-member Facebook group 'Women Helping Women Entrepreneurs', was astounded: 'Seventeen minutes a day? Amazing!'

Others echoed the sentiment:

This sounds too good to be true!

Now you're talking! Everybody can find seventeen minutes a day!

Wow. That sounds so doable!

That's incredible! I've been plugging away at a book for over two years... Sounds like I need your training!

Was anyone unhappy that I hadn't shared the *how*? No, it was a free training, and they gathered value from getting one of their main book-writing questions answered: 'How long can I expect it to take?' Me providing the answer alone (without giving the steps on how to make it happen) moved the needle—and not only that, but it piqued the interest of those serious about getting started, to the point where they reached out for further information.

So, the conclusion is this: even if you feel like you're not giving value by providing only the *what* and the *why* of certain aspects of your process and the reader's journey, what you're sharing has value—and I imagine you can think of many different examples in your own experience to support this.

YOUR PERSONALITY (RAW, REAL, AND RELATABLE)

While running one of our live Q&A sessions for my clients inside The Write and Publish Your Book Mastermind, I spoke into the beauty that is sharing your true self with your readers, and how magical it can be to share who you are by being raw, real, and relatable. During this discussion on the power of showing up with potency (i.e. not watering any of yourself down, whether for social media or in general day-to-day business), one of my clients picked up on my unintentional phrasing and told me it really resonated with her. So, 'raw, real, and relatable' was born.

The conversation had come about while we were discussing the book of my late client Mary Swan-Bell. *Post-Its and Polaroids: Snippets and Snapshots of an Overthought Life* is a stunningly poignant memoir, written and published in 2020, just two years before Mary's sudden, very sad passing. The book, with its countless reflections on who we are as human beings, for better and worse, and its no-sugarcoating approach to the sharing of anecdotes, was so beautifully captivating, emotional, and inspiring that it amassed incredible reviews and rankings across all major book platforms, including Amazon and Goodreads. Mary's wit, humour, and sarcasm combined with her desire to be honest and transparent and 'hold a mirror up to herself and others' in the telling of her memoir was embraced wholeheartedly—and she was loved and appreciated for it.

Could people have judged the way these real-life stories unfolded? Of course.

Could Mary have potentially been called out for how fearlessly she told her truth? Absolutely.

Could she have been chided for sharing family secrets or 'airing her dirty laundry'? Quite possibly.

But none of that happened, because it was evident, from page to page, that Mary was not only incredibly compassionate and empathetic, but deeply concerned with unapologetically embracing 'her human' (the good and the bad) and honouring the truth of everything she had lived.

This is the epitome of a memoir.

The result? A total of 101 ratings and a score of 5.0 on Amazon; 60 ratings on Goodreads and a score of 4.5; and readers across the world sharing the impact of this book:

> *I was immediately drawn to the author's intense ability to connect with thoughts that rattle around in my head, as if she'd taken up residency there. Internal & external battles I've fought in my own life spill out in her pages in a familiar way, but with a different and always better vantage point.*

> —LORI
> *Amazon reviewer*

> *I love the way the author reminds us of an unconscious truth, that is—where we are and who we are now is perfect!*

> —EMMA GRANT
> *Goodreads reviewer (and one of my clients)*

135

Reading this book felt like sitting in front of the fireplace, drinking a bottle of wine, and sharing stories with one of your dearest friends. Not quite an autobiography... Not really a self-help book. This is journey of an incredibly insightful woman as she careens through her life, growing psychologically and spiritually. Pulling no punches, telling her story with honesty, precision and courage...

—IRVING KUO
Amazon reviewer

Her humour and honesty [are] exactly what I like in a book and a friend. She made me think about things in my own life. I'm still pondering how to be a better parent, friend, and co-worker, thanks to her perspectives.

—LISA BELLIN
Amazon reviewer

I share these reviews here because sometimes, the fear of telling our deep truth or showing ourselves in a not-quite-perfect light can be daunting and scary, and it all too often elicits fears surrounding what people might think or say, or how damaging sharing might be. But there is also the other side to that coin—the really incredible, transformational, life-changing side that can have a very real impact on people and the way they live their lives.

Readers feeling heard and understood.

Readers considering how they can become better parents and better in all relationships.

Readers identifying themselves as perfectly imperfect and right where they need to be.

That's incredible stuff.

Rereading these reviews even now in the moment that I write this chapter moves me to the point of tears and induces real heartache for Mary no longer being here. At the same time, however, it's incredible to recognise the way a book can leave its mark and shape you—Mary's book as a case in point.

Your book can have that same impact.

Of course, Mary's book is a memoir, not a lead-generating non-fiction, but the lesson still stands: sprinkling your book with true insights into who you are—the highs and the lows and your soul-level truth—can not only prove to be really quite special for those looking to you for guidance, but also pivotal in tightening the bond between you and your reader. It also allows your journey to be documented and your teachings to be remembered, forever scribed onto the page and sent out into the world. It's a legacy.

For this reason, it's so important that you show up unapologetically as true selves; with a real potency, with no element of who you are watered down. It's so important—and your readers will appreciate and value that. And maybe even it will move them.

Be potent in all you're sharing.

Once upon a time, Mary told me she was 'scared to death', but also that she 'knew her little book needed to be out there'. I'm so proud of Mary for feeling the fear and doing it anyway, and so glad she saw it through. And you can do the same thing.

Be potent in all you're sharing.

What's incredibly powerful to remember is that, what could feel vulnerable or even difficult for you to share can be a beacon for someone else; you can be their lighthouse and hope. Sometimes, *painful* for you can be *powerful* for someone else.

So, be potent in all you're sharing.

REAL LIFE STORIES: PERSONAL AND PROFESSIONAL

This follows on from the above, but requires its own little section, because there is the common question (at least as voiced to me by my clients) of whether a business book should include personal stories, or whether a memoir can ultimately lead back to business.

Let's be honest, people don't just buy into the service and results, but into you as the person behind them. There are countless business coaches, fitness instructors, publishers, book mentors, financial advisors, and the like, but none of them have your very own combination of expertise and personality.

This is why in all our offers—whether our mastermind program, our blueprinting program, or even in the case of our ghostwriting clients—I constantly emphasise the importance of getting your reader to know, like, and trust you. There may be other professionals in your niche who are, on paper, offering the same product or service as you do, but they are not *you*. They do not have your backstory; your way of talking; your way of doing business; your way of connecting with others. People remember you not for what you did for them, but for how you made them feel.

In mind of all of this, it seems intuitive to deduce that you should include as much of your backstory—the context and circumstances behind how you have gotten to where you are now—as possible, and this is an accurate assumption—and yet, simultaneously, it is also an inaccurate assumption.

Allow me to explain.

I have previously mentioned Scyller Borglum, one of our clients (and an absolute powerhouse at all she does). In her book *Study Habits for the STEM Student: Every Habit you Need to Succeed in Your STEM Courses and Degree Program*, she makes a point that I believe can be applied to all things business, and is especially relevant to your lead-generating non-fiction: people want to hear about the baby, not the labour pains.

This, I think, perfectly summarises the balance between 'personal' and 'professional' that needs to be struck in your lead-generating non-fiction. It is important to be personable, yes, and should a certain event, circumstance, or interaction have formed the very basis for why you do what you do now, it is pivotal that you include this, insofar as it relates to you and your story as a business professional. What *isn't* relevant is a) all the gory details—the moments of frustration and glory; the highs and the lows, in technicolour detail—of that story; and b) every other event, circumstance, or interaction that is *vaguely* connected to how you got here. Keep it concise and focused. Emotion is essential. Personability is essential. Vulnerability is essential. Waffle is not. In fact, it is unforgivable. It will not be appreciated by your editor, nor by your fast-moving, action-taking target audience. It suggests an inability to 'read the room' and a tendency to overshare.

This very same discussion has arisen on different occasions inside my mastermind, which have then expanded into a discussion on my own experiences with domestic violence. Those particular experiences were the catalyst to me launching my publishing house (my dream business) in 2013. So then, the question arises: is that piece then relevant?

The answer is: yes. Sharing this experience highlights that my publishing house isn't just a business, but something far more important at a heart and soul level. It's also not just a *job*, but something I choose to do every single day in my pursuit of a life lived by design. Furthermore, as we know, it's super-important that we develop know, like, and trust by showing who we truly are at our very core. Sometimes, that comes from sharing the difficult times (as long as they are relevant), as it's essential our audience is shown the more human side of us (not just the business side).

What *wouldn't* be relevant is every single detail from that time of my life, or other parts of my past that arguably, yes, have all led to me being where I am today, but do not have a *direct* association with my company. I may have certain traits because of certain experiences I had on the playground, but that doesn't mean they need including in my lead-generating non-fiction. Save that for your memoir—or just your personal journals. Your readers do not need to know every microscopic detail of your life in order to know, like, and trust you.

Think of the authors, influencers, thought leaders, business owners, and celebrities you trust, admire, and feel connected to. You probably know the key points of their life that brought them to what you know them for now, whether that is the journey behind the founding of their company, the 'breakthrough' role in their acting career, or the story that led to the formation of their brand, but you probably do not know the more miscellaneous details of their life (unless, as a superfan, you have sought these out yourself!). The same applies to your reader: they need to know about the things that will allow them to get to know you through the lens of what you do in your work. Anything beyond that is surplus to requirements. Remember, your book is not about you; it is about your reader.

The importance of having a personable writing style also cannot be overemphasised. Plagued by imposter syndrome, my clients will often feel the need to write their book in a very formal, academic tone. If this is your natural writing style, by all means, proceed; your editing team will be able to tweak so that the writing is warm and personal but professional. If, however, it is not—if you love 'flowery', wordy writing with sprawling descriptions; if you love to write with colloquialisms and dry humour, punctuated with short, quippy sentences; if you love drawn-out metaphors, allegories, or for-instances—take this moment to bulldoze any walls you have built around yourself, and fully lean into your preferred writing style. Readers (and media consumers in general) love something that feels fresh, authentic, and unique. So, go the full hog with your natural writing style, and enjoy the knowledge that this very authenticity will make your readers warm to you that much more—no oversharing needed. You will still need plenty of client case studies and testimonials (we'll discuss that next), and you will still need lots of personal anecdotes for demonstrative purposes (again, only the anecdotes that will move your reader forward), but you will not need to figure out how to blend 'memoir book' with 'business book'. Keep the *what, why*, and *how* business-focused and geared towards helping your readers move from Point A to Point Z, but keep the delivery authentic to who you are—and watch the superfans roll in!

Share who you truly are at your core, and allow yourself to very naturally interweave that into your content, *without* sharing the stuff that doesn't directly pertain to your company. Don't label something as 'personal' and, subsequently, 'does not belong in my business book', but still evaluate every inclusion with a critical eye, especially if the content is very personal and/or sensitive. Ask: Will this move my reader forward? Does this enrich what I am teaching? Is this something I would share at a conference, in front of hundreds of strangers? If you are still unsure, ask a trusted friend, family member, or business contact—or, better, your editor.

CLIENT CASE STUDIES AND TESTIMONIALS

Writing and publishing a book on your chosen topic positions you as an expert in your field, because the implication underpinning the effort and investment is that if you were dabbling in this arena, you surely wouldn't have enough content about it to write a full book, nor would you invest significant time and money into it. That being said, simply writing a book isn't enough: you need to boost and elevate your authority as much as you possibly can by sprinkling in client case studies, testimonials, and real-life, in-business examples. This will help your readers to trust that whatever process, strategy, or goal you're helping them to move through and achieve, you're equipped to lead them to that success because you've helped other people to do the same.

Showcasing the 'wins' of your clients is also insanely helpful in allowing your readers to unpick the belief that you're some kind of unicorn, and that that's why you've achieved all you have. In other words, it demystifies your process. Yes, you're special, and yes, you're skilled, and yes, you excel in an area your audience does not. However, you're not a magical creature who was born with an innate gift to achieve *x*, *y* or *z* without any guidance whatsoever; you're a normal human being who simply took the steps to learn and implement—and if you can learn, your audience needs to understand they can, too. By providing your readers with details of your own journey coupled with the journeys of your clients, your reader is able to look at you way up on the pedestal they may have positioned you on and truly see that (in the kindest, most loving way) you're not special, and that if you and all your clients can do this, they can, too.

The danger of simply talking about your own journey from Point A to Point Z is that your prospective clients might be more inclined to think that your success was a fluke, or that you're 'different', or that embodying something doesn't mean you can teach it. You can instantly alleviate (and even altogether eradicate) this thought by showing how you've helped others just like them.

In addition, including your client 'wins' and achievements in your book is just plain nice. It shows gratitude for each and every one of them. Without your clients, you wouldn't have a business, so it can never hurt to make your clients feel appreciated and cared for and like they did the right thing by choosing you.

Again, it's all about casting that net of impact as wide as possible.

As an additional bonus, those clients you mention might even buy a copy of your book knowing you mentioned them, which is a nice sweetener if you're pursuing any kind of professional Bestseller status (see Chapter 12).

More than anything, though, let's shout our clients' names from the rooftops just because they deserve it.

CALL-TO-ACTIONS

What kind of lead-generating book doesn't incorporate actionable next steps and key resources to allow your reader to make even more progress on their journey? One that epically fails at fulfilling its potential!

A few years ago, I published a post online that spoke into the value of a lead-generating book and made reference to 'subtle lead-generation throughout'. This inspired someone in my circle (someone whom I knew had already written and published a book on her field of expertise) to message me and ask exactly what I meant by this. When I explained, she responded with absolute horror that she hadn't known she should do anything in her book to direct readers to her, next steps, or additional resources (even just social media); she had instead only spoken into solving the problem her clients wanted to solve.

Honestly, in that moment, my heart broke a little. This was a highly esteemed and well-known professional in her arena; someone who had achieved much success and scaled her business; someone who had been told that the next step would be to write and publish a book, but wasn't given any guidance on how best to do that or any education on how to position and leverage it to grow her business.

I emerged from that conversation feeling so sad for her; for the wasted time, energy, and potential.

Of course, I offered to take her through the relaunch process, with emphasis on making sure the book would be positioned to attract and nurture leads into her business, but she never took that step.

With this said, it's imperative that throughout your book, you allude to your products and services so that your readers feel safe and secure in the knowledge that, should they need or want further help, it's available to them. These subtle references can be made throughout your book, but should not be focused on *selling* your reader. Your focus should always be to give your reader what they relative to the moment they're in, while providing the assurance that further help awaits.

Some readers won't wait for any explicit instructions, but will reach out straight away with a request of how they can dive straight into your highest possible level of help. I personally behave like this as a client myself, and welcome the clients that show up in my world in the same way.

As an example of this, I was recently listening to the audiobook version of a book written by someone in the 'money mindset and abundance' space. In the first 600 words (the Foreword), she had spoken to me in such a way that I knew what the book was going to deliver and what I could expect from her paid offers. My next course of action wasn't to listen to the rest of the book, but to pause the book, go and follow her on every social media platform I could find, buy into her low-ticket programs and courses (so that I could get a taste of her program content and its platform and delivery, ready for me to move into higher level offers), and then resume the audiobook. That book turned me into a complete superfan (as I have discussed in great depth inside my mastermind) because the references to what her next level of help looked like really spoke to me, so I didn't need to hang around or wait to find anything else out.

Even in our publishing house, this happens often: someone will reach out to me after seeing my content or getting word-of-mouth referral, tell me they need (for example) ghostwriting, and sign up on the spot, because they know what they need and that I can provide it. I even recently had someone send me a DM that said nothing more than, 'I'm interested in your publishing house offer.' Short and sweet. She knew I was taking high-level women through the process of launching and scaling a million-dollar publishing house in a year, and simply reached out for the next steps.

Of course, your book will always attract some readers like that (and some will absolutely show up in that way), but others will take more time, need more nurturing, and be more slow-and-steady in their progression through the steps and decision-making before they reach out. Your job is to make sure there is something to cater to both types of reader and client across all sections and chapters of your book: the fast movers and the simmer-and-percolate type. Both are amazing, so both need the right call-to-actions.

A FOREWORD THAT SETS THE SCENE

As noted in the preceding section, a good Foreword can prove to be incredibly lucrative for you and your book. It can introduce the reader to who you are (through both personal and professional lenses), the authority you have in your space, and all that's to come and all that you offer.

Some prioritise having someone well-known write their Foreword for them (commonly a form of 'pay to play'), and of course that's fine if that works for you, as well-known names can help you to make a lot of noise and build up hype during book marketing campaigns. However, for me, it's super-important that whoever writes any Foreword for any of my books knows me well, knows what matters to me at a heart and soul level, understands my mission and what it means to me (way beyond business and money), and can speak into the most important things about everything I do: integrity, standards, and expertise.

A well-written Foreword can make a huge difference to how a reader feels about you way before they've even read your own words, and it presents an opportunity for you to be shown in a light you might not necessarily have stepped into yourself. Take the example I provided earlier: when I read that particular Foreword, I had no idea who the writer was; I had never heard of her, nor did I know her work. Nonetheless, it succeeded in positioning the author as an authority in her space. It took me from a cold lead who was listening to a random audiobook suggested on Audible, and transformed me into a warm client who intentionally put myself in her world and generated significant revenue for her company.

That's what it's all about. That makes a good Foreword, and that's what a good Foreword makes.

My advice here would be to not chase someone with a huge name in your arena (unless you know them personally, of course), but to choose someone who can pour truth and authority and the 'wins' they've experienced onto the pages. That's infinitely more important.

LEAD-GENERATION AND LEAD-NURTURING THROUGHOUT

When writing lead-generating books—books that provide value and seek to help our readers as they progress on their journey way after finishing the book—it's absolutely critical that we make sure the book is able to work for us. Although this has been touched on in Chapter 3 (Book = Booked) and will be detailed in greater depth in Chapter 13 (Making a Book Work for Your Business), it's nonetheless super-important that the value of lead-generation and -nurturing, and its critical role in making a book successful, is reiterated.

Over the years, it's been quite shocking to me quite how many people I've spoken with, whether via DM, email, or on alignment calls, who have written and published books without any conscious consideration as to how they can not only generate leads from their book, but also nurture those leads from book to business. It's such a missed opportunity.

Your book needs to be working for you, even when you don't, and that means generating leads and directing those leads into your business. It can only do that if you have very intentionally detailed what further steps can look like for your reader; what they can do to get on your email list, such as taking advantage of an additional free training or high-value PDF; how they can take the next steps to work with you, such as by scheduling in a call or sending a direct message or email; and what they can expect to invest (even if just providing a range, such as high five figures).

Without telling your reader there are additional steppingstones available to them on their journey, what those are, and how they can take them, they will simply read your book, take the value from it, think it was great, and be done with it. Maybe they'll remember you and that book you wrote, but that doesn't necessarily help your business to grow. So, you want to provide very clear instructions as to what your readers can do to benefit from additional free or low-cost help and support, and subtle references to the higher-ticket, larger investment solutions.

Note the very intentional wording there: *very clear instructions* for the free and low-cost steps; *subtle references to the larger investment solutions.* Why? Because your reader has already invested in you: they have chosen to direct money, time, and energy to you and your book, so the last thing they will want is to be pitched to; put in a corner and hard-sold. That doesn't benefit anyone. Rather, your book needs to be centred on providing value, moving your reader forward, and delivering ultimate value by presenting the next steps should they want to *progress* further. Note that it's a choice—*their* choice—and they can, if they so choose, take the value from the book and do nothing more. However, if they operate differently and want to progress as far as they can as quickly as they can, it's important they're provided with the tools needed to facilitate that.

What I think is really important to highlight here is that, when you don't provide your prospects with next steps, you ultimately do a disservice to them and all they've invested in you. This is not too dissimilar from the companies we occasionally stumble across that make it feel really difficult to pay them—my husband and I discuss this often—

and how there's nothing more frustrating for a customer. 'We want your product! We want your service! Why can't we find where to go to get it and how to pay you? Don't these companies want money?' It's exactly the same.

I see this often in the entrepreneurial bubble in which so many of us operate; we see people talking about their offers and their services, but there is no clearly signposted route for what we need to do to take advantage (and, no, DMs and calls simply aren't comfortable for everyone). Clear, easy, simple avenues need to be available—and, notably, avenues that don't mean more work for *you*, as the business owner.

Make it easy for your readers. Show them the way. It doesn't mean they have to take it. You're simply providing them with the information they need to make an informed decision—and that is your job as the author of your book.

WHAT NOT TO INCLUDE

This section requires far less explanation (if any), but is still critical to your book's success (if we're defining 'success' as leading warmed and nurtured readers into your business).

TOO MUCH OF THE HOW (LEADS TO OVERWHELM)

As already discussed in greater depth in Chapter 6, it's essential to be very clear and intentional when it comes to those aspects of your programs, services, and products you provide the *how* for in your book. Specifically, you want to be certain you do not provide too much of the *how*. Not only can this prove to be overwhelming for your readers, but it can also completely negate the need for them to take your relationship further by working with you more closely.

With this said, be sure to provide the *how* behind only three to five micro problems, without giving away too much of the gold relating to the key pieces of your flagship or super-high-level offerings. The biggest transformational pieces need to remain a secret, reserved for your high-level clients, with the book merely alluding to them.

As examples:

As a publishing house, our flagship service is the professional publication and global distribution of our clients' books, and during the process of transforming a client's rough draft into a globally available hardcover book, paperback book, e-book, and audiobook, we undertake quite literally hundreds of different steps and processes. Imagine if we were to provide the *how* of all these different steps; the dozens and dozens of steps we lead our clients through with editing; the dozens of stages of cover design; the countless steps for the overall publication! Not only would the book resemble a college textbook, but it would also succeed in completely overwhelming our readers while at once negating their need to work with us.

Not helpful at all.

As another case in point: when creating our Successful Book Publishers: Complete Business Model™ program in the first quarter of 2023, we came to document more than 300 different go-to trainings and tutorials to guide our clients on everything from establishing a publishing house all the way through to positioning books as International Bestsellers. Of course, since this was a comprehensive 'plug and play', 'business in a box' model, much of the training is delivered in a 1:1 capacity, because to do so in any other way would be completely overwhelming for our clients. However, the point remains that if we were to document all of that process in a book, it would end up being more of a tome than a standard read, and I can't imagine many of our clients being able to see the process through.

In summary: you should not include anything so detailed, comprehensive, or lengthy in its execution that the overwhelm could paralyse your reader and cause them to quit.

Less is more, truly. Fewer steps, more action, greater results.

BAD CLIENTS

Yes, we've all had them. Yes, we could probably talk and talk about the scenarios underpinning those experiences, why the client was so bad, how you'd never work with them again, and so on. But to detail them in your book could result in legal ramifications.

Of course, you can absolutely reference experiences without mentioning names or providing identifying information as a way of helping your readers to disqualify themselves if they have the same tendencies, but that's very different to slating someone to the high heavens while not expecting a lawsuit for libel.

I mention this only because I've witnessed this scenario a number of times and had to gently guide my clients away from being sued from multiple angles. My advice? Praise the amazing clients and leave the bad ones in the past.

TRADEMARKED PROCESSES OR COPYRIGHTED INFORMATION

Do not include in your book anything to which you do not have the rights or which you have not been given explicit consent to share. Be diligent in establishing what is and isn't public domain, what falls within the remits of fair usage, and how much of someone's work you can reasonably share (with reference to them, of course) without leaning too much on someone else's efforts.

Notably, a good publishing house and good editors will flag any reference to works that might need to be queried so as to avoid problems in the future, but you, as the author, are still ultimately responsible for what you share and what is ultimately published. If in doubt, do research, seek legal advice, and communicate with the original creator/copyright holder. If you remain unsure, leave it out. Your book can and will be great without it.

YOUR OWN CATHARSIS

It is common for people to want to write books as a way of communicating and working through their emotions and giving those emotions their own dedicated space. While I completely understand the want (and sometimes need) to brain-dump certain experiences onto the page, it's essential that as an author and authority in your space, you are mindful of your readers when digging into the emotions and using your book as a means of catharsis.

As we have covered and depending on the concept of your book, what you do in your business, and how you help your clients, it might be absolutely vital that you dive deep into what you have experienced, such as in the case of trauma, as this can help your readers to feel safe in the belief that you know how they feel, as you've navigated something similar. However, it is critical (as with all content you share in your book) that everything you share is done so in mind of your readers. With this said, allow this thought to guide you when sharing:

> *Everything you share must move your reader forward on their Transformational Journey.*

You've got to strike a balance between sharing to move your readers journey forward and sharing just because it's a catharsis for you. There is a need to be very, very clear and very intentional about that. If you're unsure, always ask yourself: is it relevant?

> *Everything you share must move your reader forward on their Transformational Journey.*

For further guidance on this, see 'Real Life Stories: Personal and Professional' above. The takeaway from this is that, although it may sound super-obvious, we have to share our experiences in a way that allows our Dream Clients to gain something from it; to benefit in some way. It has to move them forward, either in terms of their journey or in building their relationship with you. If what you're sharing doesn't do that—if it's purely an emotional outlet for you—don't share it with your readers. Journal it. Put it down on the page, by all means, but not on a page that's intended for your reader's eyes and their transformational journey.

> *Everything you share must move your reader forward on their Transformational Journey.*

The balance comes down to being very careful that we don't overshare and that we keep things at a level that moves our readers forward, without emotionally dumping on them. Also always be sure to set the scene and gain permission before sharing anything that could be potentially upsetting by highlighting the context of what's to come and providing a trigger warning if there are any details or more visual elements. To catch your readers unaware won't be a positive thing for them or you.

Everything you share must move your reader forward on their Transformational Journey.

So, although writing a book can be cathartic as a whole, be sure not to use the process as a catharsis as your overarching objective. Remember: your book is not about you. It's about your reader.

ACTION STEPS: CHAPTER 7

1. Write a list, from memory, comprising what you *should* be including in your book.
2. Write a list, from memory, comprising what you *shouldn't* be including in your book.
3. Re-read this chapter and note down the other *for inclusion* and *not for inclusion* elements you may have forgotten. Drill these in!
4. Repeat, write down and ingrain into your mind (print out and display somewhere visible if you need a reminder): *Everything I share must move my reader forward on their Transformational Journey.*
5. Start brainstorming:
   o What micro problems could you solve throughout your book?
   o What could you share that helps with the know, like and trust factor, i.e. raw, real, and relatable?
   o What CTAs might you include?
   o Who springs to mind first when you think about who could write your foreword?
6. Share your key takeaways for Chapter 7 inside the Facebook group: www.facebook.com/groups/entrepreneurbooksuccess.

CHECKLIST: CHAPTER 7

1. Wrote a list of what should be included in the book.
2. Wrote a list of what *shouldn't* be included in the book.
3. Re-read Chapter 7.

4. Ingrained into my mind: Everything I share must move my reader forward on their Transformational Journey.
5. Brainstormed high-value and critical inclusions.
6. Shared my key takeaways for Chapter 7 inside the Facebook group.

CHAPTER 8
UNIQUE LEAD MAGNETS AND RESOURCES

IF YOU JUST KEEP PUSHING AND KEEP TRYING, THEN
EVENTUALLY YOU'LL REACH YOUR GOAL.

—NAOMI OSAKA
World No. 1 Singles Professional Tennis Player

I AM A HUGE FAN of the inclusion of unique lead magnets and of a Resources page at the back of your book. Both of these provide your readers with even more value than they initially expected to get from your book.

To dig into free lead magnets first and foremost: lead magnets are additional, exclusive content, such as free downloads, high-level trainings, and so forth, that have been intentionally crafted for your readers. In other words, they are additional pieces that are not available anywhere else—not to your mastermind clients, your 1:1 clients, or your course students.

Not only does the inclusion of unique material make your readers feel special (and accordingly incentivise them to buy your book, almost like they're being invited into a secret club), but it's also a strategic and no-brainer business piece offering several benefits, as we will see shortly.

Furthermore, a Resources page at the back of your book is a really helpful go-to for your readers. This page very clearly details exactly where your readers can go to get extra help, whether complementary or paid. More on this shortly, too!

EXCLUSIVE LEAD MAGNETS

GATHERING LEADS FROM YOUR BOOK

Additional free resources that are sprinkled throughout your book can, as one key benefit, allow you to very clearly identify which of your new leads have come from your book.

As an example, consider someone buys your book on Amazon. At this point, because they've gone through Amazon (and therefore provided Amazon, not you, with their name, email address, and shipping details), you would never know that you have a new lead or someone new in your world. Even if they were to then follow you on social media, you would still never know that they had come directly from your book (unless, of course, they reached out and told you so). But imagine if you had a unique, free resource that was exclusive to your readers. They go to this resource, input their name and details, grab the free resource, and— *ping!*—end up on your list. You would then know that that particular person has bought your book, because they have the book-exclusive link.

You would then be in the amazing position of having a totally new list of warm leads—'warm' because they've already bought your book and therefore taken your relationship to the next level by excitedly joining your mailing list. As a result, you would then be able to nurture them further with very specific book-related email sequences.

TRACK YOUR READERS' PROGRESS

Your unique lead magnets also facilitate you being able to keep a record of where your readers are at in your book, again positioning you to provide really valuable nurturing and further help going forward. Allow me to explain:

Imagine that your book is your stage—a platform from which you're able to directly speak to your audience about everything you can do to help them achieve their dream results. Through your book, you're essentially giving a presentation and handing out one tool after another after another (i.e. the *how* of the three to five micro pain points you have decided to address in your book). Then, imagine periodically inviting members of your audience up onto the stage and giving them the opportunity to get closer to you and work with you in a more high-touch way, whether a complementary hot-seating, 1:1 coaching—whatever this offer or opportunity might look like for you. Your audience would absolutely jump at that.

Think about how every time you provide a tool to your reader, you can essentially invite them up onstage to get a little bit closer to you. That is, throughout the course of your book, you can provide somebody with a strategy that helps them to solve a micro pain point, and then give them some kind of high-value resource, whether a training, a live video... something they can go and claim through a simple opt-in form and then get that much closer to you through.

That benefits everybody.

As an example, let's take my free resource in Chapter 1 of this book. Every time someone signs up for that particular resource, I'll know they're at Chapter 1 in this book, thus allowing me to then customise any outreach. (Note: This is where tech support comes in; see Resources for some incredibly valuable resources to help you streamline the processes in your business.) Now imagine they're at Chapter 9 and taking advantage of a high-value training that talks to them about a pivotal step in the journey. Maybe this stage signifies the perfect time for you to be introducing yourself in a very real way and setting the stage for your relationship going forward. So, consider how valuable it would be to be able to reach out via email or, even better, phone, to discuss the current and next steps in the journey.

Essentially, unique lead magnets can enhance your reader's progression from Point A to Point Z, give them even more value than they ever expected when they bought your book, and allow you (as the authority) to reach out when you know they're at certain points in their journey.

To me, this is a complete no-brainer, and something all authors of lead-generating books should look to incorporate into their plan.

MY RECOMMENDATIONS

I would advise brainstorming anything and everything you can give away for free that could potentially move your reader forward and encourage them to move the relationship they're building up with you 'off the page'.

What's important to remember here (just as with all the content provided in your book) is, you want to be giving as much value as you can, with a focus on solving three to five micro problems, while ensuring you don't overwhelm your reader. Accordingly, choose one additional resource you can incorporate into your book for each of the pain points you are providing a solution for. In this way, you will be offering three to five solutions and three to five corresponding resources. This doesn't mean including resources just because they're a 'good idea' or would be really cool to incorporate, and then haphazardly scattering them in. They need to be very intentionally thought through and strategically placed, to align with the content being delivered to your reader at that time.

To help get your creative brain engaged, some ideas for additional resources might include:

- A free demo/service trial (for those in the tech and automations niche). This could be named *The Amazing Time-Saving Automation Machine*.
- A workshop or a training (for those in the parenting niche). This could be named *How to Get Your Baby to Sleep Through the Night*.
- A roadmap (for those in the business niche). This could be named *From Cold Lead to High-Ticket Client: Your Organic Funnel*.
- A To Do list (for those in the digital products niche). This could be named *From Idea to Launched*.
- A discovery call (for those with a business program).
- A checklist (for those in the publishing niche). This could be named *How to Know When Your Book is Finished*.
- A sample chapter of another book you have published, or that you have in the works.
- A worksheet or workbook (for those in the book-writing niche). This could be named *My Book-Writing Progress*.
- Audio files (for those in the manifestation niche). This could be named *Meditate Your Way to Abundance*.
- A sales letter or template (for those in the sales coaching niche). This could be named *Our High-Converting Organic Sales Funnel*.

- A physical mailer (for those in the greeting cards niche). This could be named *Free Greetings Card Sample*.
- A discount (for those in the home furniture niche). This could be *25% off All Sofas*.
- A physical freebie (for those in the beauty niche). This could be *Handmade Soap with Lavendar Blossom*.
- Relevant contacts (for those in the marketing niche). This could be named *Our Little Black Book of PR Contacts*.

Obviously, some of the above examples might not be applicable to your specific niche or the book you choose to write, but they still may inspire some ideas for what you can offer your readers.

One critical factor to consider when formulating lead magnets is obviously the cost. How much is it going to cost you to incentivise your readers to opt in?

Of course, the value of a lead-generating non-fiction is that your leads will pay to become leads, so I would always encourage you to choose additional resources that don't cost you anything to deliver (beyond the work required to create them in the first place) and that are of a 'one and done' nature (i.e. you create them once and then do not need to tend to them going forward).

When providing discovery calls and physical freebies, for example, there obviously is a cost incurred in these cases, so it's important to weigh this up. With some businesses, it may be a no-brainer to provide a real taste of your product or offer, such as if you own a coffee brand, so this investment would be worth it.

Whatever it is you choose to incorporate, the most important thing is to ensure it's highly valuable and aligned with where your reader is at, the pain points you're looking to help them solve, and the stage they're at in their transformation. If this is done well, your offer will feel irresistible: they will jump at downloading the (exclusive) additional value being presented.

As a further point: make the process of downloading or accessing these additional resources super-quick, simple, and easy so that it becomes a no-brainer, and be sure to guide them on what steps they need to take to do so. For example:

If you're interested on digging a little deeper with how your book can help you to generate millions of dollars through you reducing your book's distribution availability, you can grab our FREE Million-Dollar Distribution Formula by visiting:
https://www.entrepreneurbooksuccess.com/MDDF

Remember: 1 micro problem = 1 resource.

As another point of importance: make your landing pages and systems as professional as possible. How you do one thing is how you do everything, and so the quality of not only your resources but the way in which they are delivered is paramount.

As an example, I like to make sure that our publishing house academy's PDFs, onboarding sheets, and processes are immaculate, so I have processes and automations in place to facilitate me in providing clients with customised PDFs and seamless, automatic onboarding into our academy programs. Professional standards, seamless access, and no delay between client payment and their receipt of the paid-for product/service are all critical. Going the extra mile like this echoes the quality and standards we align ourselves with in everything we do in my company, regardless of whether we're mentoring, ghostwriting, or publishing, and it's encouraging for our clients to see this reflected across all platforms.

So, I would encourage you to invest some time and effort (even if this means outsourcing the tech and automation side of things) so that all of your book's additional resources are accessible and delivered in a way that's reflective of your brand and company overall. It's a worthwhile investment.

ADOPT DIFFERENT MEDIUMS OF DELIVERY

Nowadays, there are many different platforms and mediums through which content can be delivered to us. As a natural result of this, people tend to have varying needs and wants with regards how they digest their content. Thus, I often advise my clients try to deliver their additional resources through several different mediums so that they can essentially cater to all their clients. More specifically, I recommend providing additional resources of varying media, such as one resource in the form of an audio file, another resource as a video, and then maybe a downloadable

PDF (for reading). You might consider providing a checklist to get people writing, or maybe a manifesto for that constant visual reminder that sits in the subconscious.

Keep your reader in mind at all times, and it's all so much easier.

THE RESOURCES PAGE

Your Resources page is a go-to place for when your reader is looking for any and every reference to further help you have made in your book. It also provides a type of action plan for their next steps. While the instructions are not quite as explicit as this, a Resources page still essentially implies, 'Download all these goodies, follow me on social media, schedule a call, and then sign up for our mastermind.'

Importantly, you want to be directing your readers to the Resources page from the very beginning of your book. By so doing, your reader will be aware of its existence way before they reach the end of the book. This is critical, since even when they *do* reach the final chapter, they might not read the very final pages (the content beyond that last chapter). By very clearly telling your reader where they can find high-value resources at a glance, they will know exactly what they need to do in order to work with you in a much more in-depth way—without them having to go back through previously visited content.

Use this checklist to guide you on making sure you include everything your reader could possibly need or want after reading (or, in the dreamiest of scenarios, while they're reading):

- Free Resources: Every lead magnet and additional component you've offered in your book should be provided in list form. Provide the resource's title, where it was originally detailed, and where your reader needs to go in order to gain access.
- Paid Resources: Every product and service you've referenced in your book should be provided in list form. Write the type of resource it is (e.g. a twelve-week program), complete with where your reader needs to go to sign up.
- Social Media: List any usernames and links to platforms you commonly use and are active on, such as LinkedIn, Facebook, and

Instagram. Having easy access to your social media will allow your readers to quickly jump into your real world and immerse themselves in it, so make this step easy for them.

- Websites: Detail all the websites you have and how your readers can subscribe to any newsletters.
- Email Address: Should you be happy for your readers/prospective clients to email you, be sure to add an email address here. This can prove really powerful in moving people from book to business.

Take a look at the Resources page at the back of this book for an example of how yours could look.[3]

ACTION STEPS: CHAPTER 8

1. Brainstorm unique lead magnets for inclusion in your book—one for each of the micro problems you're helping to solve.
2. Share inside the Facebook group any ideas you've had: www.facebook.com/groups/entrepreneurbooksuccess.

CHECKLIST: CHAPTER 8

1. Detailed a handful of lead magnets to mirror the micro problems I will help my readers to solve, with each lead magnet designed to help them make progress.
2. Shared my ideas, epiphanies and key takeaways on Chapter 8 inside the Facebook group.

---

[3] I would recommend that you do not include details of the investment so that you are able to recraft, restructure, and reprice offers without worrying about the fact you have solidified pricing in your book. If you do not plan on changing any aspects of your offer in the future, however, you might see value in detailing price points so that your readers are better qualified as they move into an 'off the page' relationship with you. Whatever works best for you works best.

CHAPTER 9
HOW TO KNOW WHEN YOU'RE FINISHED

'BEGIN AT THE BEGINNING,' THE KING SAID GRAVELY,
'AND GO ON TILL YOU COME TO THE END: THEN STOP.'

—LEWIS CARROLL (1832–1898)
Author; quoted from Alice's Adventures in Wonderland

I AM OFTEN ASKED THIS question: 'How do I know when I've finished and it's time to submit my draft to you for editing?'

Even up until recently, I haven't really known how to answer this— how long is a piece of string?—but after working through this with a client on a mastermind call, I came to create a checklist, which has proven to be applicable and a lighthouse for all my authors.

I'm providing that checklist here.

What's important to stress beforehand is quite how valuable this checklist truly is. It's gold. Don't underestimate it in allowing you to move forward. Allow it to provide you with a true compass; a clear roadmap; a definitive guide. The alternative is to ponder, review, correct, self-edit, and do all the things that will keep you stuck in having a first draft and never making progress.

I've seen it and spoken into it on many different occasions, but perfectionism is the thief of progress, and striving to make the manuscript 'perfect' before sending it off to your editor or publisher is a never-ending task. It can go on into forever.

As an example, I currently have a client who I have had for several years (yes, *years*). We must have had a dozen different versions of her 'final' manuscript, if not more, and any time she gives us the go-ahead to move to publication, something else crops up and requires that she completes yet more work on the manuscript.

I realise, just as my whole team does, that there's probably fear at work here—fear of finally putting those words out into the world, fear of success, fear of backlash—but, regardless of the rationale behind this seemingly never-ending cycle, the pursuit of perfection is keeping her rooted.

This is one reason I encourage you—*urge* you—to take this checklist and properly align yourself with it. Send it off to your publisher and trust in them to do the job you've hired them to do; to make your book the very best version of itself. That's their role. You provide the first draft; they'll do the rest. If they're a good, skilled, and experienced team, they'll communicate with you very honestly about what can and should be done to make your book go from good to great, whether that involves structural edits, the incorporation of new content, the removal of other content, or the sharing of more value (or less value). Stick to the checklist and trust in your team, and the rest will be golden.

Remember: success loves speed.

THE CHECKLIST

1. Solved Three to Five Micro Problems:
   If you have solved three micro problems (not key pillars of your business or program offering), your reader will have received huge value.
2. Completed the Transformational Journey:

Have you successfully moved your reader from Point A to Point Z? Has your reader experienced a transformation? Your business will do the rest.

3. Included Case Studies and Results:
   Have you showcased the results you help your clients achieve and built authority and status by sprinkling in case studies throughout?

4. Been Raw, Real, and Relatable:
   Have you shared your personal journey? Have you showcased the highs and the lows? Your readers need to develop know, like, and trust.

5. Included Offers and Action Steps:
   Your readers will self-qualify, but they need details of your paid offers (subtle references) and free offers (direct references), and links.

6. Sought Colleague/Friend Feedback:
   Seek feedback from someone who knows your niche/journey/mission who can highlight any further inclusions that may be needed.

I have also taken the liberty of providing you with a printable checklist so that you can keep this visible and in mind as you progress through your journey.

You can access this here:

www.entrepreneurbooksuccess.com/finish.

Remember: when you have the foundational pieces in place, as detailed above, your book will have all it could possibly need. Your team can handle the rest, whether through navigating the publication process for you—complete with all the editorial and content-related work you could need—or even through Hybrid Ghostwriting. Regardless, your team is your greatest asset during the book-writing and -publication process, so try to trust in them and why you hired them. It'll keep you making progress at all points.

ACTION STEPS: CHAPTER 9

1. Access, save and print out the How to Know When You Are Done PDF (available here: www.entrepreneurbooksuccess.com/finish). Allow this to keep you moving forward with clarity and without procrastination.
2. Share any key takeaways or golden nuggets you've garnered from Chapter 9 inside the Facebook group: www.facebook.com/groups/entrepreneurbooksuccess.

CHECKLIST: CHAPTER 9

1. Saved and displayed somewhere visible the How to Know When You Are Done checklist.
2. Shared key takeaways on Chapter 9 inside the Facebook group.

PART III: SUCCESS

CHAPTER 10
ROUTES TO PUBLICATION

BE THE CHANGE THAT YOU WISH TO SEE IN THE
WORLD.

—MAHATMA GANDHI (1869–1948)
Indian Lawyer, Anti-Colonial Nationalist, and Political Ethicist

AM I BIASED?

ONE OF THE MOST COMMON categories of questions I get asked is, 'How does the publishing process actually work?'
'Do I retain the rights?'
'How do royalties work?'
'Do you handle the editorial stage?'
'Would I need to hire a cover designer?'
'Who pays for the printing of the book?'
'Does the book become available on Amazon?'
'How do I achieve International Bestseller status?'
This is usually when I explain the various routes to publication that an author can take.

Of course, as the owner of a hybrid publishing house, it would be fair for you to assume that there's going to be some degree of bias when I provide a general overview of each route to publication. However, what I will say is that it was my very clear understanding of, experience in, and insight into the industry that encouraged me to build not a traditional publishing house, not a self-publishing platform, but a hybrid publishing house. I could have chosen any of the three options available to me, but I opted for hybrid because it made the most sense (and continues to do so), from an author's perspective.

What's more, as an author myself, I've experienced exactly what it looks and feels like to navigate the traditional and self-publishing worlds:

I've been the writer who received rejection letter after rejection letter before eventually giving up.

I've lived through the overwhelm and feeling of being so completely out of my depth as I moved through the self-publishing process, editing my own work, designing my own cover, and trying to understand print-appropriate files, metadata, and distribution. I have also lived through the humiliation of the inevitable 'book flop' that comes when you 'wing it' like this.

It was as a result of these experiences that I not only threw myself into the theory of the publishing industry (and also got industry experience for seven years way before I launched my own company), but I also experienced the industry as an author way before becoming the CEO of a hybrid publishing house.

Nonetheless, in this chapter, I provide my own view of the publishing world, which directs attention to the different routes available to you, as an author, and the various (subjective) advantages and disadvantages of the different models.

Without question, there are benefits and drawbacks to every approach, but ultimately, the decision comes down to what you and what you prioritise:

What do you want to achieve?

In what period of time do you want to be published?

What does book-related success look like for you?

What type of finish and standard do you want your published book to have?

Importantly, there is no right or wrong answer to these questions. It all comes down to you, your goals, your business, and how aligned you feel with each approach. Again, my role is only to present the information—the facts, if you will—and to leave the ball in your court.

THE DIFFERENT MODELS

TRADITIONAL PUBLISHING

As an overview, traditional publishing is probably what we all think about and imagine when we consider publishing our books. Essentially, traditional publishing involves a publishing house taking an author's manuscript and completing all the stages of publication for them. One might argue it's the epitome of a done-for-you service. The different processes undertaken by a traditional publishing house generally include editing (line edits, copyedits, and proofreading), typesetting (the formatting of the interior of the book), cover design, publication (making the book available in all formats), worldwide distribution (availability across retailers), and some marketing.

All these processes are carried out to the highest possible standard, whether cover design or copyediting. So, as its main advantage, traditional publishing provides the author with the knowledge and security that their book is going to be really well looked after and that the finished product will be absolutely impeccable.

As an additional advantage, you will also not be required to pay out of pocket for any element of the publication.

However, the road there is long and difficult. Securing a traditional publishing contract first requires that you find a literary agent. Your literary agent will then send a sample of your work (whether a synopsis, an in-depth outline, or the first few chapters) to publishing houses. Should the publishing house be interested in the material they've reviewed, they will then request the full manuscript. It is upon reviewing the full manuscript that they will then decide whether to take on the author or, ultimately, reject them.

If a publishing house does indeed decide to offer a contract, the author may or may not be provided with an advance on their royalties. This tends to happen if the author is well-known, if they have a significant social media following, or if they own an already-established brand.

Royalties present an area where the disadvantages of traditional publishing can be seen most clearly, in that it is more common than not for authors to receive 5%-10% of the book's royalties (their publisher retains the rest). This is viewed as the publisher's 'reward' for not only the risk they have taken by publishing the book (because there was no guarantee it would sell), but also for undertaking all the processes involved and their corresponding overheads and expenses.

As another key drawback, authors also lose all rights to their project, and, with that, complete creative control. This means that when a traditional publishing house contract is signed, the publisher then own the rights to the work, meaning they can change anything and everything they want to.

As the bottom line, you'll emerge from a traditional publishing contract with a professional publication you can be incredibly proud of and that hasn't required any direct financial investment from you, but this will be many years in the making, and in the end, you won't own the rights to your work.

For me as a business owner and entrepreneur, I could never and would never forfeit my rights. I want to be sure I'm in control of where my book is being sold, when it's being sold, its price point, and whether I can use it as a springboard to propel me onto a well-known streaming platform or talk show. I also want to be adequately compensated for the time and energy I've invested into my own book, rather than allowing a publishing house to benefit to the tune of millions for my own hard work.

The future value of your book is, quite simply, unquantifiable. The direct sales of services from your book, the speaking events and opportunities stemming from the book, and the leads that go on to become clients, all create a profound and wide-reaching ripple effect of sales that will just continue and continue. With that said, handing over rights and royalties to a publisher really doesn't align with me—and obviously hasn't aligned with my clients.

> *I tried to get published for ten years. Ten whole years. The rejection was all-consuming, and I was so downtrodden. It was so easy to lose sight of what I was doing it for—so that people could read my book—and I almost did. Thankfully, there are other ways, and they don't take the sacrifice.*
>
> —ERICA VOGUE
> *CEO of BrightSpark Training and Mentoring*

Considering the above, fast-forward ten years and ask yourself:
Will your book still be relevant?
Will it still be able to create the impact you want?

Traditional publishing houses can offer an author an exceptional standard of publication and global distribution, but authors being required to forfeit all their rights and the vast majority of their royalties means there really is a lot of weighing up that needs to be done: is the trade-off worth it?

SELF-PUBLISHING

As someone who has previously navigated self-publishing and who sees people go through this process every single day, I would say that self-publishing will always be a route to publication that I highly recommend professionals to *not* take.

Although it's possible to be successful through the self-publishing route, ultimately, this requires expertise in several different areas (if you are to make sure your book is the very best version of itself). It doesn't take a rocket scientist to realise that if publishing a book really was as simple as Amazon's self-publishing platform would have you believe, there wouldn't be large, incredibly successful publishing companies across the world with vast departments dedicated to every single stage of the publication process.

Yet many people tell me that someone (or many people) in their orbit has advised them to 'just self-publish on Amazon... It's free and so easy!' Amazon's three-step process grossly undermines everything that needs to go into a high-quality publication, and it's predominantly for this reason that I cannot get behind self-publishing. These shortcuts are degrading to the overall quality of books and the publishing industry as a whole, which honestly breaks my heart. My advice would always be to not take advice from someone who suggests this unless they've been through the process, achieved an exceptional standard of output you yourself would be thrilled with, and been successful in the ways you yourself would measure book-related success.

Nonetheless, self-published books can look and behave the part. They can look good (if done in the right way), and they can provide an additional stream of leads and revenue for a business. However, getting to that level of success requires the ultimate resource (time)—and a lot of it.

Let's imagine you have been able to invest hundreds upon hundreds of hours of time into learning everything there is to know about the editing process, then cover design, then typesetting (interior layouts and formatting), and then the different formats of publication, global distribution, and marketing: it still remains that one of the most popular and commonly used and widely available self-publishing platforms is significantly lacking with regards the overall quality of production.

Despite Amazon being the biggest retailer in the world and its initial business being centred on books, the printing and overall standards of Amazon's self-publishing platform are, in 2023, subpar, to say the least. Although I am an expert in the field (meaning I know exactly what to look for to identify whether a book has had a professional, experienced publisher behind it), it is still worth mentioning that I can see a mile off when a book has been a self-published—and not only that, but printed by Amazon. The telltale signs are visible at a glance, and they can be so damaging.

When it comes to entrepreneurs, coaches, mentors, and professionals specifically, the most important thing to know is that self-publishing will cost you time. That time will most commonly be spent in research, and this research will leave you with an ultimate decision: do you learn how to self-publish well yourself, or do you find experts that you *think* can do the job well for you? This becomes a classic case of the blind leading the blind, because if this isn't your own zone of genius, how are you ever going to know that someone else is operating in *their* zone of genius?

This, sadly, was something a good acquaintance of mine, Kim Beadman (wife of jockey Darren Beadman), reiterated to me during our time together at a business retreat in Australia:

> *I have written and published a book, but I self-published it. It was an absolute nightmare, and I would never do it again. Next time, I'll be going with you.*
>
> —KIM BEADMAN
> *Life Coach and Author of* Born to Thrive

This sums up the self-publishing process, and underpins the fact that when moving through that process, you will have to take a huge leap of faith on who is the expert:

Who is a good editor?

Does this cover designer know what it takes to create a good cover?

Does this so-called typesetter know how to format a book well?

How can this book be made available worldwide and in retail stores, not just on Amazon?

Again, it all comes down to what you prioritise in your business and for your book, and in complete honesty, if you are looking to travel the most inexpensive road, your business may not be in the right place, right now, for you to even be considering writing and publishing a lead-generating book.

In this same vein, one aspect of the self-publishing journey I am always very vocal about is the fact that more often than not, the poor man will pay twice. That is, it's highly likely that you're going to pay more than once for every single stage of the process if you don't hire a professional team right off the bat.

Let's take cover design as an example. If you were to hop onto a freelancing platform, such as fiverr.com, and hire a cover designer, it could be that when that cover design lands in your Inbox, you find yourself not only disappointed but absolutely devastated at the quality, wasted time, and wasted investment. If you draw the conclusion that your cover designer is really not up to scratch or hasn't understood the brief, and their output is therefore really not aligned with your vision for the book and the business you've built, you will then have to hire another cover designer. If all goes well, this one might be great and good enough to use. If not, you will have to keep on navigating this process over and over and over until you can arrive at a cover design that embodies everything you were wanting.

Now imagine going through this for every single stage of the publication process. Not only would this cost you in time, energy, and stress, but it would also cost you significantly more money than if you were to secure an expert in the first place.

One of the most important things to say when it comes to self-publishing is that if this is not your area of expertise, I can pretty much guarantee your book will ultimately not be aligned with industry-wide publishing standards—and if this ends up being the case, any reader of your book (you don't need to be an expert in the publishing arena) will be able to tell your book has been self-published. This is something I discuss with people every single day: it's super-easy to see when something is 'off' with a book, even if you don't know exactly what's wrong.

In the entrepreneurial space, where we're looking to make sure that everything we put out there is reflective of the standards we align ourselves with in the provision of our products and services, it is imperative that every aspect of our book—the content, the reader's journey, the cover design, the editing; every single thing—is absolutely on point. This is critical when you're striving to make sure your readers-turned-clients can feel confident that the standards you bring in your business are exactly where they need to be. In other words, if your book lacks quality (whether in printing, overall production, or any area of the publication process), this will negatively affect the perception your Ideal Clients have of you and your business. Why? Because how we do one thing is how we do everything.

To balance things out, what I will say is that self-publishing allows you to retain complete rights to your work and a very high percentage of royalties. If we look at Amazon, for example, authors are given up to 70% of the book's royalties, and complete rights to their work. The drawbacks, however, centre on a profound lack of quality across all areas if you're not working with experts to help you navigate the different processes.

In conclusion, self-publishing is the right option for those who are willing to invest significant amounts of time in learning how to move through the various publication stages to achieve an exceptional standard of quality, but who do not want to financially invest in their book. Essentially, it's the perfect fit for somebody who prioritises money over time, and who is happy for quality to be the lesser priority of the three (time, money, and quality).

HYBRID PUBLISHING

Hybrid publishing, from a completely unbiased perspective (and what I mean by that that is, from the standpoint of someone who is a writer themselves), is the option I, personally, would always go for, simply because it provides a middle ground between traditional publishing and self-publishing. Essentially, it provides the advantages of both models (namely, complete rights and complete royalties, as is available to those who are self-publishing, whilst also ensuring the standards of publication are absolutely exceptional, as would be achieved through traditional publishing).

Decades ago, hybrid publishing houses were referred to as 'vanity presses', simply because there was a trend where if somebody was rejected by a traditional publisher, they could then pay to publish their work instead. These days, with the advent of technology and a multitude of different platforms and middle grounds becoming available to many different industries across the world, hybrid publishing is becoming more and more commonplace and more warmly received, predominantly owing to the fact it makes the most sense in a number of different situations and for many different demographics, such as entrepreneurs and business professionals who prioritise speed and quality simultaneously and recognise business investments as just that: investments. Nonetheless, it's still common for older generations to view hybrid publishing as 'vanity publishing', and to declare that people should run as fast as they can if a publisher asks for payment, without actually considering the fact that all methods of publication cost money (with traditional publishing potentially costing the most in publisher-retained royalties).

The bottom line is, in the professional sphere, hybrid publishing will always make the most sense, and is widely embraced by very well-known thought leaders and influencers—so much so, in fact, that even some of the biggest publishing houses in the world have begun to offer hybrid solutions.

For business professionals, emphasis tends to be on achieving high standards of publication and global distribution, and speed. This approach to business expansion and the recognition that success loves speed ultimately presents a no-brainer for forward-thinking business owners who view books as a key piece of their marketing and lead-generation strategy.

The key benefits of hybrid publishing are, as an author, you are able to achieve the same standards of publication as those offered by traditional publishing houses, whilst retaining complete rights and complete royalties. In addition, hybrid publishing houses tend to be able to move through the process an awful lot quicker than traditional publishing houses can, not to mention the peace, confidence, and security that comes with having all the necessary professionals available to you all in one space.

All these reasons are why I initially created and launched (and have since, over the past decade, nurtured, polished, and refined) our boutique book publishing house. For my Dreamy Clients, the hybrid route just makes sense. We provide a turnkey solution that brings together the expert knowledge that needs to be poured into creating the perfect book across all its many elements and facets, and which offers the freedom that comes with complete rights, complete ownership, and 100% of all royalties.

When it comes to the disadvantages: there is the need to invest in your book in order to initiate the process. However, I have had clients echo my own thinking that this actually isn't a drawback, because the cost to publish is far less expensive than either trying to source professionals yourself or selling your soul to a traditional publisher.

To take this one step further, if we were to consider the fact that through traditional publishing, an author would forfeit as much as 95% of their royalties, again, it makes complete business sense to go the hybrid route. If you're able to earn more than the investment of hybrid publishing in royalties, it ultimately makes far more sense to go hybrid so that you can retain your rights and then receive 100% of all royalties. This means that when your initial investment has been recouped, you are completely in profit. And this is without taking into account the fact that we make money from the book as a result of sales *from* the book, not sales *of* the book!

When opting for hybrid, the potential is huge. Not only are you prioritising time and quality, but you are investing in future profitability by retaining your rights and directing revenue straight into your business, without any outside party intercepting any percentage.

IN CONCLUSION

To sum up, whichever route to publication you take, there is nothing more important than making sure you seek out professional help and advice to allow you to get things just right and to minimise the mistakes made along the way.

Remember: when your book is sent out into the world, there is no clawing it back. Even if you were to remove it from distribution, there will always be copies floating around, complete with errors or any poor reflection of your services. It really, truly does pay to cut a check and get it right the first time.

ACTION STEPS: CHAPTER 10

1. Learn the key differences between self-publishing, traditional publishing, and hybrid.
2. Look at how your goals align with each of the publishing models available. Which do you think calls to you most? (Remember: there is no right or wrong answer.)
3. Share inside the Facebook group any gold you've stumbled across and what you've learned in Chapter 10:
   www.facebook.com/groups/entrepreneurbooksuccess.

CHECKLIST: CHAPTER 10

1. Gained an understanding as to the different publishing models.
2. Established which model I think might be best suited to me, my book and my business.
3. Shared key takeaways on Chapter 10 inside the Facebook group.

CHAPTER 11
THE PRE-ORDER WINDOW

IF I CANNOT DO GREAT THINGS, I CAN DO SMALL
THINGS IN A GREAT WAY.

—MARTIN LUTHER KING JR. (1929–1968)
Leader of the American Civil Rights Movement

THERE IS NO REAL NEED for me to delve too deeply into pre-order marketing, as marketing, in and of itself, is a beast I would always encourage you outsource to experts (unless you are one yourself; in that case, go for it). Plus, self-marketing is most often completed by those opting for the self-publishing route, and my hope is that after reading this book, you will see the value and importance of professional publication (not self-publishing).

Nonetheless, it's important I include a chapter solely focused on this topic, however short, because pre-order marketing is one of the main problem areas I see on a daily basis when it comes to other entrepreneurs and professionals who are self-publishing books.

It isn't that self-publishing authors are doing the whole pre-order thing wrong; they're not doing it at all.

Even writing those words here—*they're not doing it at all*—is so completely mind-blowing to me. They've spent their time, energy, and money doing what I am forever encouraging people to do (writing and publishing a book), and then when it comes to the all-important pre-order stage, they take the shortcut and head straight to Publication Day.

Why? Why?!

I've seen it probably every single day that I've worked inside my publishing house for. I've seen the posts and emails that start to lead up to the moment quickly gathering speed and accelerating towards the finish line. In a matter of hours, the content goes from something along the lines of, 'I'm so excited, I've just approved final edits from my editor!' to, 'I'm so excited, my book is being published *tomorrow!*' It's incredibly frustrating, and I have to fight the urge, every single time, to reach out to the soon-to-be author and plead with them not to speed through this final stage. But, of course, I don't, because a) it'd be unsolicited advice, and b) let's not put a dampener on their experience.

If you take nothing more from this chapter than the general premise underpinning the next pages, I'll be good with that, and that is:

An eight-week pre-order period is a must!

Eight weeks. Just under two months. It's really not forever, but it can be so pivotal to your book's success—and I'm not only talking about the interest and pre-order sales you can generate in that time, but the most practical, strategic parts (and in fact, I would argue this is the most important aspect of the pre-order stage).

An eight-week pre-order period is a must!

I'm talking about giving your distribution network time to list all the details pertaining to your book: the cover image, the page count, the publishing house, the price point, the author name... all the key metadata. This can take time, even if we do live in a modern, technologically advanced world. It still takes time for all the key retailers in the world to receive and publish all the information they have in relation to your publication. As an example, I've known Amazon to take anywhere between twelve hours and six weeks to do this.

An eight-week pre-order period is a must!

And then what if something needs changing? What if there's a typo in the book's long description? What if the cover image isn't displaying (and note that this can take several days to work its way across the network)? Not to mention the process of linking e-book listings with paperback listings, which should, in theory, be an automatic process, but rarely ever is (and therefore requires that you liaise back and forth with retailers to get the two editions detailed on the same book listing).

An eight-week pre-order period is a must!

Now consider going to publication *tomorrow* and people buying your book, to find it's riddled with errors. Or the cover hasn't printed correctly. Or any other number of possibilities. Wouldn't you want to have the time to order a proof copy, go through it with a fine-tooth comb, highlight anything and everything that needs changing, and then update the files—*way* before anyone gets their hands on a copy?

Wouldn't you want to then give that second proof copy to your team, or to someone you trust, to highlight any other errors?

An eight-week pre-order period is a must!

It happens, believe me. Even world-renowned publishing houses have errors and typos creep into their manuscripts (I'm sure you've read books with errors; this might even be one of them!). It's par for the course. And that happens when those publishing houses and their extensive editorial teams have already done a pre-order period, already done the ordering of proof copies, and already examined the physical book rather than just the on-computer version. Imagine if they'd sent it straight out into the world without those checks and without that time! You'd be devastated.

An eight-week pre-order period is a must!

Take the time to go through everything, and don't panic when there are things that need changing: if your website is wrong on the back cover; if there's a header missing on page 149; if there's a formatting issue. This is exactly what the pre-order stage can be used for: to polish and refine, and be sure you're happy with everything.

An eight-week pre-order period is a must!

Not to mention: it's just good practice and it just makes sense.

Now, with the above said and hopefully resonating deeply (because I can't imagine you ever wanting to rush through the final stages and sending a 'less than' book out into the world), let's consider what the pre-order stage should look like for you, regardless of whether you are self-publishing or working with a professional team.

Essentially, it should look productive; it should be full-to-bursting with marketing, even if you're not a pro. As also touched on in Chapter 13 (Making a Book Work for Your Business), I would advise completing at least one marketing activity every single day in the leadup to your pre-order period, whether that be an email, a social media post, a live, or a reel. It can be anything. It could mean sending out press releases, booking podcast interviews, scheduling campaigns, sending review copies, or running a free training in a group (your publisher will be better able to guide you on what this can look like, with you working together as a team and aligning your efforts). The most important thing is to talk about your book, make noise, and make sure people know about your book. You don't want your book to be the world's best kept secret, so be sure your ideal market knows it exists.

ACTION STEPS: CHAPTER 11

1. Remind yourself aloud: *An eight-week pre-order period is a must!* Remember this especially if you opt for self-publishing. Don't allow overexcitement to kill your launch.
2. Share any key takeaways or golden nuggets you've garnered from Chapter 11 inside the Facebook group: www.facebook.com/groups/entrepreneurbooksuccess.

CHECKLIST: CHAPTER 11

1. Committed to reminding myself that an eight-week pre-order period is a must. A non-negotiable.
2. Shared key takeaways on Chapter 11 inside the Facebook group.

CHAPTER 12
INTERNATIONAL BESTSELLER STATUS

SOME PEOPLE DREAM OF SUCCESS WHILE OTHERS
WAKE UP AND WORK HARD AT IT.

—NAPOLEON HILL (1883–1970)
Bestselling Author

INTERNATIONAL BESTSELLER IS A STAMP the most authors would love to achieve at some stage of their journey as an author. For entrepreneurs and other professionals specifically, this 'trust stamp' and status piece seems to have become a non-negotiable in recent years, and this ostensibly stems from the abundance of '#1 International Bestselling authors' constantly filling our feeds, whether on Facebook, LinkedIn, or other platforms.

As the CEO of a publishing house, I know and understand the ins and outs of achieving International Bestseller status. I know what it takes to get there, how it works, how to achieve it, and what it can mean for your business. I also know and understand what it *doesn't* mean, what it *doesn't* rely on, and what *not* pursuing it can do for your business. In the interest of giving you, my readers, an all-encompassing view of the publishing process and how it can help your business grow, I will be diving deep into the truth of this highly regarded, widely pursued, highly prioritised shiny object.

Can I help you to achieve this if you work with me? Absolutely. It's guaranteed as a part of our service.

Would I recommend it? Quite honestly, no.

That being said, there's also no shame or judgement should you seek to add this to your portfolio of accolades and entrepreneurial wins. My only concern here, in this chapter, is that I give you the full picture and speak from the heart as someone who is not only invested in the publishing industry as a business owner, but who is invested in the book industry as a complete book-obsessive. My objective is to continue to be a trailblazer in this industry and change how things work for the better, and one step in that direction is to put it all out there as we discuss International Bestseller status: the myths, the facts, and what those oh-so-glitzy Bestseller badges truly mean.

WHAT EXACTLY IS 'INTERNATIONAL BESTSELLER'?

When a book achieves 'Bestseller' status, it is recognised for having appeared on the bestseller list of a particular platform, such as Amazon or *USA Today*. In essence, the premise of the bestseller list is that it displays the top-selling books for that particular week—though, notably, that is not always the case (more on that to come). For our purposes, we can say that bestseller status signifies a large volume of sales taking place within a short period of time.

In the same vein, 'International Bestseller', put simply, means 'bestseller' rank has been achieved across two or more territories or countries. For example, if a book features on the bestseller list on Amazon.com (U.S.A.) and Amazon.co.uk (U.K.), it can then be considered an International Bestseller.

Accordingly, when *The Wall Street Journal* or Amazon see a spike in sales in a particular category, they look at which books in that category have sold the most copies during a predetermined period and assign bestseller status to them. For Amazon, their bestseller charts go all the way to 100 (meaning you can be the 100th bestselling book in a particular category that week and be recognised as a bestseller), while *The New York Times* has various lists, which are broken down into 'fiction', 'non-fiction', 'print', 'eBook', 'paperback', and 'hardcover', with between fifteen and twenty publications being detailed on each list. *USA Today*, on the other hand, has a list of 150 titles.

WHAT 'INTERNATIONAL BESTSELLER' *ISN'T*

During the past ten years spent running my publishing house, Onyx Publishing, and its various imprints, I have come to learn so much about the various bestseller lists, how they work, how they *don't* work, and how things truly look behind the curtain.

It has to be said: there is a lot of smoke and mirrors in this particular area of writing, authorship, and publishing. Accordingly, it's only right that we dig deep into correcting some of the common misconceptions and making sure there is complete clarity going forward, because if you don't truly know how something works, it's near impossible to make a plan for how to achieve it.

As such, in the following sections, you'll find an overview and breakdown of how each of the more well-known bestseller lists work. It is my hope that this provides some understanding as to what needs to be done to achieve these status pieces (should you wish to pursue them), as well as what isn't reasonably within the average person's control.

THE MAIN LISTS: AN OVERVIEW

THE NEW YORK TIMES *BESTSELLER LIST*

Whenever I talk about *The New York Times* Bestseller list, whether inside my mastermind, to 1:1 clients, in groups, or even during free trainings, one thing I commonly witness is absolute shock—shock to a jaw-dropping degree—when I share the truth behind it... and that truth is that *The New York Times* Bestseller list is not a *bestseller* list, but an editorial list.

What does this mean? Well, in simple terms, the titles featured are those which have been handpicked by an editorial team, not those which have sold the most during the preceding week. Although the precise details of how titles are chosen is not known (this has been referred to as 'trade secret', with the rationale for this apparently being 'making sure authors, publishers, and marketing entities cannot cheat the system'), what *is* known is that fewer than a handful of individuals in the news surveys department of *The New York Times* are responsible for the selection, *not* the book review department.

Perhaps we should actually refer to *The New York Times* Bestseller List as *The NYT* Editorial list?

Other uncommonly known facts include the following:

-   Although sales data is used as indicating factor to direct attention to books that are creating a lot of noise and generating interest, the very small team in the news survey department choose which books they think *should* be on the list, without consideration of sales numbers.
-   The books on the list don't get read, simply because it would take far too much time to read all the contenders. As a result, only an overview (i.e. a review of the blurb, title, subtitle, cover, and preliminary chapter) is completed for each book.
-   You can outsell the titles featured on *The NYT* list and still not feature on it.
-   So much of the decision making comes down to who you know. If you can get your book in front of someone in the news survey department, you stand a far better chance of being considered for the list.
-   *The New York Times*, as an organisation, has its own goals, objectives, and agendas, and so the titles they choose for their list will be aligned with those.
-   The top-ranking book of the week might not even be the highest selling book. Again, it doesn't come to sales figures; it's an editorial list.
-   Self-published titles rarely ever feature on the list. As such, if you plan on taking the self-publishing route to publication, it would be highly advisable to remove *The NYT* from your sights so as to avoid inevitably disappointment.
-   You're far more likely to feature on the list a second time than if you have never been featured before.
-   There is no link between quality and whether a book is (subjectively, of course) *good*. You can write and publish an incredible, well-reviewed, popular book, and it still probably won't feature on *The NYT* (editorial) list (unless it has been picked by an

editorial team, of course—but then at that point, the quality was by the by).

What's genuinely quite heartbreaking about sharing the truth behind this so-called 'bestseller' list is that so many people (fiction authors and entrepreneurial non-fiction authors alike) feel like the earth has fallen from beneath their feet when they are told. Being featured as a *New York Times* Bestseller is something they've often been dreaming about for the longest time (and something that would potentially have been used as the yardstick for their success). I've had clients with *The NYT* bestseller emblem pinned to a vision board above their computer system, as something they see and use every single day to keep them inspired and moving forward. I've heard people tell me how if they never achieve anything else in their life after achieving *NYT* Bestseller, they'll be happy.

Now, don't get me wrong, it's not impossible to achieve this high level of 'gold and shiny', but the truth of how the system works means it's a lot more difficult to attain than simply putting together a solid marketing and sales strategy and focusing on selling 10,000–15,000 units in a week. The fact the list is editorial in nature, with a team's opinions ultimately deciding who features on the list in any given week (not to mention business lunches and personal relationships being behind so many of those decisions), means securing a position is that much harder and that much more out of reach. This ultimately makes the route there a lot less clear (think blurry and fuzzy—visible, but with the direction beyond the horizon all but impossible to make out). That's because, quite simply, sales are not the deciding factor.

AMAZON BESTSELLER

Amazon Bestseller is one of the most commonly and, importantly, *easily* achieved International Bestseller status pieces. Although more and more people are learning how to achieve a rank that means they can claim being a bestseller into eternity, it still doesn't seem to be losing its perceived value.

To me, this feels kind of strange.

To speak into this more: when liaising with new clients, it's common for one of their main questions to centre on whether we can achieve this rank for them. Furthermore, despite the huge number of leaders in the entrepreneurial space claiming this status, it continues to be voiced as not only super-important but critical to their definition of success.

Of course, every writer, every author, every client, every entrepreneur, has their own definition of book-related success, but as the publisher responsible for my clients' successes, it's incredibly important for me to communicate exactly what pursuing this badge of honour can mean—and what it doesn't mean.

So, what it *does* mean:

It *does* mean that once your book has hit any rank in the top 100 of any of Amazon's categories and retained that spot anywhere in the top 100 for a minimum of two hours, you can claim to bestseller status.

It *does* mean that if you secure bestseller status in more than one country, you can claim International Bestseller status.

It *does* mean that you can retain this title forevermore. You can shout it from the rooftops until the cows come home.

It *does* mean you will likely receive some degree of recognition and additional status when communicating to people that you are a bestseller (because you don't know what you don't know, and the *perception* of Bestseller continues to be cast in a prestigious light).

There are also what I would argue to be the most important pieces, and those pertain to what bestseller status *doesn't* mean:

It *doesn't* mean that your book has sold a significant number of copies. Rather, it means there has been an influx of copies sold within a short period of time. Bestseller status is not synonymous with having sold a ton of copies and now being able to book a five-star trip to Barbados.

It *doesn't* mean an abundance of opportunities and doors opening, especially within the entrepreneurial bubble (which is full of other business professionals who are drowning in social media feeds full of bestseller-related news).

It *doesn't* mean the work stops; that you can now hang up your 'book marketing' cap.

Essentially, Amazon's International Bestseller status symbol is not exactly as it would seem, and when you combine this with the ease and simplicity with which the status can be attained (not to mention the fact that more and more people are now placing their books in completely irrelevant categories as a means of 'cheating the system'), the badge is now, in reality, less prestigious than ever before.

With that said, however, the active, very determined pursuit of this award has not showed any sign of slowing. Even when I explain to my clients exactly how this works—what it means and what it doesn't mean—many make the decision to continue on with its pursuit, potentially because they don't want to be the one entrepreneur in their entrepreneurial bubble that *hasn't* achieved this status ('Won't they wonder why *my* book hasn't achieved #1 Bestseller when everyone else's has?'). With this said, inside our publishing house, we incorporate Amazon International Bestseller status as a guaranteed part of our service, simply because we recognise how important it is to our client base. (We even have a program that teaches how to achieve this, should this be something you'd love to incorporate yourself.)

For me, I personally and professionally measure book-related success using other KPIs (see Chapter 13: Making a Book Work for Your Business). For those who really value bestseller status, however, we are more than happy to position them to achieve this sought-after trust stamp.

USA TODAY

USA Today is recognised as one of the key bestseller lists in the United States' publishing industry, specifically because those books featuring on the list are recognised as having made significant sales within the country. Second only to Amazon, *USA Today* is known to be the second easiest bestseller list to hit, owing to its focus on sales units rather than any other factor, such as inside relationships or editorial picks.

To secure a spot on the *USA Today* Bestseller list, an author must sell around 10,000 copies of their book during the pre-order period, with only those sales made in the U.S.A. counted. Furthermore, while the list ranks the top 150 bestselling books, the top 50 seem to be recognised as the most significant.

As a publisher, I would argue that *USA Today* is one of the most important of the bestseller lists to try to hit, predominantly owing to the fact it focuses on audience reach and actual sales rather than any other potentially easy-to-influence, baseless factor. However, as a drawback, some of the books that make it onto the list can be lacking when it comes to quality and standards of publication—predominantly because it's all a 'sales and numbers' game. In this vein, sales over quality can mean the list attracts a lot of self-published works, without the emphasis on quality and alignment with global publishing standards.

THE WALL STREET JOURNAL *BESTSELLER*

Much like *USA Today*, achieving *The Wall Street Journal* Bestseller can prove to be quite a simple and straightforward goal to achieve, again because the focus is primarily directed on sales made in the U.S.A. With this said, it therefore just takes a good marketing plan and strategy to generate the required number of sales in the leadup to publication.

Although more selective in the books that make it onto the list (for example, the books are usually non-fiction and, more specifically, tend to fall into the 'business' category), they allow books from all types of publishers to feature, whether traditional, hybrid, or self. However, quality is key across all aspects (editing, typesetting, cover design, and so on), with the standards of publication needing to be reflective of those adopted by the Big 5 publishers (Penguin/Random House, Hachette Book Group, Harper Collins, Simon and Schuster, and Macmillan).

With this being said, I have seen many books that do not necessarily align with my own interpretation of 'high standards of publication' make it onto *The Wall Street Journal* Bestseller list during more recent times, and so this raises the question of whether there are, indeed, any other factors at play besides sales figures. Then again, it is my belief that a sound marketing strategy, with a goal of 10,000 sold copies during pre-order, coupled with high-quality publication, can mean success when pursuing *The Wall Street Journal* Bestseller.

SALES PERIODS

When pursuing International Bestseller across any platform, whether Amazon, *USA Today*, *The Wall Street Journal*, or *The New York Times*, each has its own period during which it measures sales. So, it's important to be clued up on this before pursuing any one (or several) of these stamps. As an example, while *USA Today* takes into account sales made during every Monday–Sunday period, *The New York Times* measures sales data between Sunday–Saturday. Then, in complete contrast, Amazon update their sales data every hour, meaning their ranks are consistently changing due to their focus on recent sales, as opposed to older sales.

Accordingly, trying to achieve a spot on all these lists at one time requires a very solid marketing strategy, with focus on every bestseller list's start and cut-off point.

WHAT DOES INTERNATIONAL BESTSELLER DO FOR YOUR BUSINESS?

There are no guaranteed results with regards 'new doors opening' once you achieve International Bestseller status. The opportunities that come can vary in several different ways, not only when it comes to the specific bestseller list you have featured on, but also what your personal and business brands are like, what your book is focused on, the niche in which you specialise, the different offers you promote, and whether there's an overarching theme or message underpinning your book.

There's a common understanding that achieving International Bestseller, such as through *The New York Times*, can create a wealth of opportunity that will ultimately skyrocket your business and your overall success, and I have no doubt that's the case. However, what I think is potentially difficult to quantify here is the growth and additional revenue certain opportunities have achieved for your business, in numerical terms. That is, it can be difficult to track how many opportunities have been brought about by your International Bestseller status, and how many would have come about regardless, *and* how much revenue these opportunities have actually brought to your business—again, courtesy of your International Bestseller status.

For me, both personally and professionally, I feel far more inclined to keep things simple and to very intentionally grow my business through a book using tried-and-tested methods, where the results are very easy to see and measure using data that's readily at my fingertips. Examples of this would be a growth in email lists with book-purchase tags and opt-ins through lead magnets I made exclusive to my book (see Chapter 8). That way, I can very easily quantify the 'success' my book has brought me. The results brought about exclusively because of International Bestseller status can rarely be accounted for in the same way.

Again, how 'book-related success' is defined differs from one person to the next, and will ultimately come down to what you want to achieve from your book, whether speaking engagements, appearing on stages across the world, or even being invited to do Ted Talks. For others, 'book-related success' might be selling 100 copies of their book every month and, as a result, bringing a handful of new, exceptionally Dreamy Clients into their business, thereby helping them to grow their revenue and perform service delivery in a more aligned, enjoyable way.

In popular culture and online, the consensus tends to be that you 'need to achieve International Bestseller in order to be successful', but, as with everything, that's just one of many possible yardsticks, and everybody's criteria is going to be different. When I look at things through not only the lens of a publisher who is very deeply invested in her clients' successes but also through the lens of a writer, I would always encourage prioritising getting your book into the hands of Ideal Clients who are going to feel aligned with you and your business; those readers who build know, like, and trust; those who will ultimately want to take steps to work with you in a more intimate capacity. Nonetheless, everyone has their own ideals and beautiful vision as far as what the results of their book can and should look like. For some clients, International Bestseller is a non-negotiable, and that's absolutely fine. I'm a firm believer that all our goals are achievable and that regardless of what they are, the right strategy and plan are the only requirements. So, if achieving *The Wall Street Journal* Bestseller is something you feel you really want or need to achieve for your book to be considered a 'success', there are definitely ways and means of making this happen, as detailed here in this chapter. My role here is only to make the facts available to you, my readers, so that you can make well-informed, well-educated decisions as to which Bestseller lists to pursue, if any.

MY THOUGHTS

Bottom line? If you want to feel like your book has genuinely been the most 'successful' and achieved what it was meant to (i.e. land in as many people's hands as possible), *USA Today* and *The Wall Street Journal* are, in my opinion, most deserving of your marketing efforts, simply because they measure total units sold.

For any International Bestseller lists and their corresponding badges (*USA Today* and *The Wall Street Journal* included) and what you want to achieve in this regard, my advice would be to get very clear on exactly which lists you want to pursue and why. If you dig deep and establish that any of these bestseller achievements are indeed nothing more than bright shiny objects and you really rationalise or justify to yourself why you want them beyond the rush of achieving them (coupled with how you might ultimately be perceived by your peers), I would encourage you to look at other ways of measuring book-related success that could prove to be far more profitable and fulfilling for you and your business in the long run.

By making sure you're super-conscious and well-informed regarding what you're pursuing and why, you'll be better able to create a plan that positions your book to boost your business and continue to work for you every single day.

ACTION STEPS: CHAPTER 12

1. Start to consider whether you would, in fact, want to pursue International Bestseller, all things considered. (There is no right or wrong answer here.)

2. Get clear on what you'll need to do to achieve whichever International Bestseller stamp you are pursuing (if any) and write these down. It pays to have an action plan.

3. Share inside the Facebook group any new information or key insights you've garnered from Chapter 12:
www.facebook.com/groups/entrepreneurbooksuccess.

CHECKLIST: CHAPTER 12

1. Made a well-informed choice as to whether or not I will be pursuing any of the International Bestseller badges.

2. Formulated a marketing strategy plan for pursuing the International Bestseller I want to achieve (if any).

3. Shared my key takeaways on Chapter 12 inside the Facebook group.

CHAPTER 13
MAKING A BOOK WORK FOR YOUR BUSINESS

I NEVER DREAMED ABOUT SUCCESS. I WORKED FOR IT.

—ESTÉE LAUDER (1908–2004)
American Entrepreneur and Business Executive

W HAT USE IS A BOOK if it isn't set up to work for you as an asset in your business? If it's not very intentionally sent out into the world, surely it will end up being nothing more than a passion project that generates a few sales, a bit of short-term interest in you and your business, allows you to list related expenses as tax write-offs, and maybe give you a little blip of excitement?

And shouldn't it be more than that?

It absolutely should—and it can, if it's set up in the right way.

When a book is set up for success in such a way where it can truly work for your business, there are a multitude of different results that materialise. For you to see these results (and for them to repeat now and into the future), there needs to be a handful of key pieces in place, not only in relation to the book, but also the author.

I get to see both sides of this coin as someone working on the inside of a publishing house every single day—the successful side and the not-so-successful side—and what I can tell you about this is that you, as an author, can choose which side of the coin lands face-up for you and, moreover, you can choose to change it at any point. So, if you're about to begin the journey and that little voice inside your head is concerned about whether your book really can do its job and help you to grow your business, allow me to tell you: it can. Even if you're well into your first draft and you're worried that not all the key pieces are in place, lean in and let me assure you: there's time to incorporate them. And if, as a worst-case scenario, you've already published your book but aren't experiencing success like you would want and you think you've well and truly messed this up, believe me when I say: it really isn't too late.

The recipe for book-related success is simple (note that, for our purposes, I'm defining 'book-related success' as your book consistently selling to ideal prospective clients who move into your business at a 5% close rate). Even if you're not an expert in marketing (which I'm not), paid ads (which I'm not), and sales (which I'm not), simply follow my advice and keep a record of the wins, and you'll soon see your book has been (and will continue to be) a worthwhile investment.

Throughout this chapter, I'm going to lead you through several different recommendations that I would say are not only complete no-brainers, but absolute musts. You might decide not to follow one or many of them, or you might decide they're all too much effort, but know that using each of these in combination will compound your results and allow you to truly leverage the power of a book in your business. And isn't that exactly what we're here for?

BOOK FUNNEL

Making your book available through a book funnel is, for me, one of the most important pieces to have in place. Does it need to be a sophisticated funnel? No. Does it need to offer a million different upsells? No. Does it need to be primarily concerned with encouraging your Ideal Clients to buy the book from you, rather than a retailer? Absolutely. Do this, and your business will steadily grow—and far quicker than if you weren't to use one.

When you add a book funnel into your business and use it to sell your book (whether the hardcover, paperback, e-book, or audiobook version, or a combination thereof), you are essentially setting yourself up to be able to maximise on three huge benefits:

- Your leads will pay you to become leads.
- You'll be able to capture your leads' details and nurture them going forward.
- You'll be saving yourself up to 40% in wholesale discount costs.
- Your customers will get a taste of your business/service.

Let me to explain each of these further.

YOUR LEADS WILL PAY YOU TO BECOME LEADS

Although this has been highlighted earlier on in this book, allow me to reiterate the power of a lead paying to become a lead, because when it's done through your book funnel, the results can be exponential.

Imagine telling a room full of Ideal Clients that you have something that's been intentionally crafted to help them to move away from their pain point (whatever it may be) and closer to their desired result. Imagine some of those people being interested enough to raise their hand and declare they want your help and that, better yet, they're willing to pay you for that help. You direct them to your book funnel, where they happily give you their name, email address, and shipping address, and then place an order for your book. Those people have not only told you they need help, but they've taken action to get that help, and now, they've paid you for that help. Forget free lead magnets and high-value giveaways: those people (who were more than likely not paying customers before) have just become customers by placing an order with you—and not just any order, but an order that clearly indicates that they need help and are willing to move now when the opportunity presents itself.

Now, whether you decide to do a Free Plus Shipping funnel (where you pay for the book to be printed and your customer pays just for it to be shipped to them), whether your customer pays the full cost of the book, or whether you're giving away a low-cost e-book edition of the book, it remains that their wallet has been opened and they have taken the first step into your world as a paying customer. It's with this intentional shift in your relationship (i.e. from a mere observer to a paying customer) that I would urge you to charge for your book—even if it's a low amount—because that payment creates a change in the dynamic: there is enough trust in you being the expert that you've been paid to offer a supportive, helping hand.

Ask yourself: When was the last time this happened—i.e. that you offered someone the opportunity to take *the first step* and they paid for it? I'm not talking about the high-ticket step, nor am I talking about someone signing up for the entire journey. I'm talking about just the *actual* first step; think DM or email. In other words, the very first touchpoint.

A book funnel not only allows you to attract those people who have the problem you're able to solve, but it very quickly moves them into the next level of a relationship: that of a paying customer.

Now imagine what could happen if, after paying for your book, they *did* have the option to take subsequent steps, such as those offered by upsells and high-value trainings. Imagine taking that client from being a cold lead through to paying customer and then through to low-ticket client, or a medium-ticket client.

There is no end of opportunity and possibility with a book funnel in place.

CAPTURE YOUR LEADS' DETAILS

Again, this has been touched on in other areas of the book, but to repeat this will mean it'll ingrain itself in your brain—or at least, that's my hope!

When you use a book funnel, you're able to capture the details of your readers, thereby allowing you to communicate with them going forward. In this way, not only are you able to clearly identify who your prospects are, but you're able to email them, offer them further help, provide more value, invite them into taking the next steps, and truly step into the role of helping those who have raised their hands and declared they want help (which is exactly what they're doing when they buy your book).

Imagine a Dreamy Client—let's call her Erica—buying your book from Amazon or one of the other key retailers, such as Barnes & Noble or Chapters Indigo. You would never even know Erica had bought your book, never mind be able to communicate with her.

Of course, when your publisher sends you a royalties report every six or twelve months, you'll see a copy of your book has been sold, but to whom? You would never know—not unless Erica herself were to reach out to you to share the exciting news. But what if she doesn't? Or what if she orders your book and, when it arrives, puts it on her bookshelf to read another day, another time, one day in the future? What then?

When your Ideal Clients buy from other retailers, you're unable to liaise with them and help them to move forward with their journey, let alone bring them into your business—and that presents massive untapped potential and lost opportunity.

For me, this is one of the golden, *crème de la crème* benefits of plugging a book funnel into your business—and it's why I prioritise directing people to a book funnel above all other retailers.

YOU'RE SAVING YOURSELF UP TO 40% IN WHOLESALE DISCOUNT COSTS

Without digging too deep into the financial aspects of book wholesalers and retailers, what I will share is that when any retailer lists, stocks, and sells your book, they expect to be compensated.

When using a professional hybrid publishing house, the main retailers in the world tend to be happy to sell your book for you at a cost of 30% of the retail price. In other words, if your book is listed for sale at $10, Amazon would retain $3 when they sell a copy. Other retailers might expect more—40% or higher.

When you sell your book through a book funnel, not only are you capturing the customer's contact information (which is so valuable), but you're also saving yourself the $3 retailers would receive as payment for selling your book for you. That means you can pass that onto your customer to make buying from you direct, through your book funnel, a complete no-brainer.

Of course, give them the option, as some customers might prefer to pay more to the likes of Amazon to guarantee next-day delivery. Many, however, will choose to go through your funnel in mind of the lower cost.

I do exactly this with my own books: I will sell the e-book edition of my book at a far lower cost than it can be found at other retailers, and then provide my audience with the opportunity to add the paperback edition on (again, at a far lower price than they would find online). This means my customers are benefitting from a screaming deal and I'm cutting out the middleman, so to speak.

Again, a complete no-brainer.

YOUR CUSTOMERS GET A TASTE OF YOUR BUSINESS/SERVICE

When your customer orders your book through your book funnel, this is where the magic can really happen, because you're able to show them what it's like to be a client inside your business.

Think a beautiful email sequence.

Think providing them with their purchase in record time.

Think directing them to your portal or academy for additional bonuses.

All of this will more deeply immerse your customer in your world, show them what it's like to be a client in your orbit, and give them a sneak-peek behind the curtain. If they feel aligned, they'll move quickly to see more of your world.

The fact is, if you can wow your customers in the very first interaction, they will want to see what else you have for them—and they'll move forward with greater confidence the next time they find you in their Inbox with a high-value offer, because they've already had a taste and know exactly what standards they can expect from being in your business.

To sum up, book funnels are absolute gold and can be incredibly powerful in growing your business, not only in terms of the leads that quickly become customers and therefore add revenue to your bottom line, but in specific consideration to the data—names, email addresses, phone numbers, etc.—that are willingly handed over to you, the expert. They're also super-simple to plug into your business (your publisher should be able to help with this as a part of your solution), ready to take and fulfil orders for you. I have seen them work well time and time again—and I've seen some books with what I would describe as questionable quality and content moving leads through to becoming paying customers and then high-ticket clients all as the result of a book funnel.

As far as your book strategy goes, I would not only advise it, but highly recommend it.

GOODREADS

As of 2023, Goodreads has an estimated 125 million active users, making it one of the largest platforms for readers across the world. As such, I would always highly recommend signing up and, when your book is published, registering as a Goodreads Author.

When I wrote my first non-fiction book back in 2015, I was very active on Goodreads, not only as a reader but as an author. Cue complete shock and awe when I found more than one-hundred people were adding my book to their TBR (To-Be-Read list) every single week. This created a snowball effect, since when a Goodreads user adds a book to their list, it's also recommended to their immediate contacts (i.e. friends and followers).

This led to me consistently receiving messages from people who had read my book and how it had helped them to achieve results.

Now, in 2023 and with just a little marketing over the recent weeks (notably while my book has still been in the pre-order stage), more than 2,000 people sit with my book on their TBR.

Goodreads is an incredibly powerful platform, and with various tools available (ads, free giveaways, and the opportunity to liaise with readers and fans), it allows you to build up a community of people who want to read your books (existing or upcoming) and who have already read your books.

In addition, Goodreads will direct people to key retailers they can purchase your book from. They also allow you to craft a unique author bio, which I would encourage you to use to incorporate a link to your book funnel. This then positions Goodreads as a part of your lead-generation strategy, by showcasing your book and directing those who are interested in reading it straight to your book funnel.

To truly maximise on this, I would advise using a unique link for your book funnel that's exclusively for your Goodreads audience. For example, while your generic book funnel might be entrepreneurbooksuccess.com, you might decide to create entrepreneurbooksuccess.com/goodreads for your Goodreads audience. This will allow you to see where your book funnel customers are coming from.

AMAZON AUTHOR CENTRAL

Amazon Author Central provides the opportunity for authors to take advantage of many different useful tools to create an incredible author hub. This can be super-valuable when it comes to showcasing your expertise in your niche and helping those who need your help to find you on the Amazon website. In addition, much like with Goodreads, you'll also be able to incorporate into your bio a unique link that will lead potential buyers to your book funnel. Although it's not always super-visible, it still pays to make it available to those who may dig through your author platform.

When I take my clients through the value of the Author Central platform (which I do through a mini training inside our academy), I note the abundance of different elements available to authors which can really help in building up the know, like, and trust of their readers. Some of these include:

- Your author photo. As the author photograph is shown below the cover image of every single book you publish, this immediately creates curiosity and intrigue for those readers on your book's listing/page. Essentially, this is the first point at which we can attract the reader's interest in who we are. The presence of a photograph encourages readers to click through to the author's page and get to know them a little more. This of course takes the author from a stranger to someone the prospective reader feels like they are coming to know.
- Your author bio. Your author bio is a fundamental element that includes a wealth of information that will help in moving your Ideal Client through the know, like, and trust journey with you. Include details of what you do, what matters to you, your mission, your cause, and where your prospective readers can find out more about you, such as on social media. Remember to also include a link to your book funnel.
- A customised URL. Otherwise known as a vanity URL, your customised URL on Amazon is now automatically created by Amazon, and tends to reflect your author name. This makes it easy for people who already know you to find you on Amazon, even with a quick search engine search. Although it's highly likely there will be someone else with your name also writing books on Amazon, it's also possible that you can grab the 'amazon.com/author' link for your name, as has been my experience. This makes everything look far more professional when you're directing people to your own space on Amazon.

As an additional benefit of the Author Central platform, it's also possible for you, the author, to gain insights into how many copies of your book you are selling in real time (provided you have an Amazon.com author account), which is always incredibly exciting. This is not generally available through other platforms, but Amazon facilitate the provision of sales reports through their link with BookScan.

DON'T PURSUE INTERNATIONAL BESTSELLER STATUS

Although I have shared my professional and personal insights into International Bestseller status in Chapter 12, it remains that this is one of the key aspects I would encourage my readers and clients to really take to heart:

Don't pursue International Bestseller Status.

Essentially, my passion in this area stems from what has been discussed with regards book funnels: when someone buys from a retailer and not your book funnel, you are unable to capture their data—and considering every single person buying your book is a potential lead and potential high-ticket client for your business, isn't it important that you be able to do that?

Let's consider for a moment the pursuit of *The Wall Street Journal* Bestseller, and let's say you decide that you're going to make it your mission to sell 10,000 copies of your book in a week in mind of attaining that badge. Those 10,000 copies all need to be sold through retailers (not your funnel)—so that means 10,000 Ideal Clients, with some Dreamy Clients sprinkled in there for good measure, are taking action to solve their current pain point, but who they are you'll never know, because they've given their name, email address, and shipping information to the retailer, not you.

Now, Amazon is able to retarget them.

Chapters Indigo is able to nurture them.

Barnes & Noble is able to sell to them.

Walmart is able to upsell them.

Not you. You don't get a look in. Not until your reader takes the book from their bookcase and actually reads the book.

Yes, your *Wall Street Journal* Bestseller trust stamp could mean opportunities for you—but what if it doesn't? And if it does, how are you going to quantify that? How are you going to be able to dig deep into the numbers and be certain that your achieving *Wall Street Journal* Bestseller was the catalyst to you being invited to a speaking engagement in front of

·

500 people?

If it were me (and it *is* me, as a writer, author, and expert in the publishing industry), I would much rather direct those 10,000 purchasers of my book into my funnel, onto my mailing list, and into my orbit, so that *I* can be the one to retarget them (not Amazon), so that *I* can be the one to nurture them (not Chapters Indigo), so that *I* can be the one to sell to them (not Barnes & Noble), and so that *I* can be the one to upsell them (not Walmart).

The thing is, we've already established in Chapter 4 that 10,000 leads could be worth US $5 million if just 5% of those readers buy into your $10,000 high-ticket solution—and so, again, I would much rather direct all of my marketing strategies into attracting the right people into my funnel, rather than sending those people to Amazon or another retailer for the sake of achieving a status that may or may not lead to opportunities.

Again, however, it all comes down to what you want to achieve and what book-related success looks like for *you*. For me, as someone leading her clients to success, I would always much rather position my clients to grow their businesses in the simplest, smoothest, but nonetheless strategic, way, and that means through a book funnel with measurable KPIs.

DAILY MARKETING

Many of my clients and many authors across the world (especially those in the business and entrepreneurial sphere) will hire PR professionals and marketing agencies to undertake their book marketing for them—and, of course, this is something I would always completely support and even recommend. However, whether you choose to hire an expert (if marketing isn't in your zone of genius) or do the work yourself, my advice would be this: complete one activity every single day that's focused on selling your book. Of course, more would be amazing, but in mind of the fact you're running a business and balancing a number of other aspects in life, and considering the fact that marketing your book on a continuous, ongoing basis is essential, aim for one activity every day and see how that compounds for you.

Your one activity doesn't need to be something super-time-intensive or costly; it could be posting on your social media, doing a quick live, sending a free excerpt out to your email list, or sending a review copy to a Dream Client. The important thing is to incorporate promoting and marketing your book into your business as a task on either your or a member of staff's schedule.

The results will be so worth it, and they'll speak for themselves. Shock horror: the more you proactively promote your book, the more copies you'll sell; and—surprise, surprise!—the less you promote your book, the fewer copies you'll sell. Either way, the results will compound.

This being said, however, if your book is set up in the right way (and what I mean by that is, if it's professionally published, if the title and subtitle have been crafted in the right way, if it's available at all of the key retailers, if it's attracting clients in through a book funnel, and if it's detailed across key platforms, such as Author Central and Goodreads), your book will organically sell itself (and I see this every single day in my business; books written and published years ago, notably in cases where the author has stepped away from their business, continue to sell—and sell well—and that's because they've been set up for success). However, this isn't to say that you should publish your book and never ever do anything to promote it ever again.

Put a link to your book funnel on the footer of your email.

Pin a mock-up image of your book as a featured post on your social media.

Direct those who can't afford your services to your book so you're still serving them.

Have your book in the backdrop of every single live you do.

Do something—anything—every day. The momentum will build, the results will compound, and your business will grow—and all thanks to your book.

TALK TO EVERYONE

Don't stop talking about your book. When I say this to my clients, some of them shrink away a little bit, but I mean it: talk about your book. How else will people know it exists?

I don't mean shoehorn the topic of your book into every conversation. I mean, when the opportunity arises, don't shy away from it: talk about it. People love to hear about other people writing books and what the journey has been like for them. 86% of all Americans want to write a book, so they're always looking to real-life examples of someone who's done it and done it well. Besides, they'll love telling other people how they met an author that day and their book was about *x, y,* and *z,* and how they've ordered a copy.

Add to that not just talking about your book, but leaving a trail of it wherever you possibly can...

One of my clients adopted a habit of leaving a business card with details of her book, complete with a QR code leading people to her book funnel, on café and restaurant tables and wherever she went, just on the off chance someone might scan the book and order a copy.

Another client would keep a copy of her book in her handbag, complete with a pen, ready to sign and give out without charge, if she happened across an absolutely Dreamy Client, such as in an airport or on a flight.

And then I, as an author myself who wants to encourage as many people as possible to explore writing and publishing a book, will consistently strive to put myself in the room with people who not only would love to write their own book, but who love to read; fellow entrepreneurs, coaches, thought leaders, speakers, and mentors. Events, whether virtual or in person, are really beautiful opportunities for you to talk about your book—and watch as those conversations turn to book sales and yet more Ideal Clients in your pipeline.

To conclude, although some might be tempted to write and publish a book, throw it out into the world, and simply hope for the best, I would encourage you (or your team of chosen experts) to do as much as you possibly can to truly make a book work for you in your business. In addition to the critical pieces that are professional publication and worldwide availability, there are also the strategic elements of making sure people know about you and your book, directing new people to your online spaces, platforms, and ecosystem, and then capturing Ideal Clients' details, before crafting a helpful and valuable nurture sequence.

All the pieces are important, and all of them help in gaining momentum in the pursuit of book-related success—whatever that looks and feels like for you.

ACTION STEPS: CHAPTER 13

1.	Reflect on why a book funnel can be so valuable and lucrative.
2.	Sign up for a Goodreads account.
3.	Sign up for an Amazon Author Central account.
4.	Commit to the process by telling people you're actually writing a book. They'll hold you accountable!
5.	Share any other insights or gold snippets you've gathered from Chapter 13 inside the Facebook group: www.facebook.com/groups/entrepreneurbooksuccess.

CHECKLIST: CHAPTER 13

1.	Decided I absolutely must use a book funnel (it's a no-brainer)!
2.	Signed up for Goodreads.
3.	Signed up for Amazon's Author Central.
4.	Started talking to people and telling them I'm committed to writing a book.
5.	Shared key takeaways on Chapter 13 inside the Facebook group.

CHAPTER 14
GHOSTWRITING

SMART ENTREPRENEURS CUT CHECKS FOR SPEED.

—DEAN GRAZIOSI
Author, Investor, Entrepreneur, and Trainer

GHOSTWRITING. IT'S A SERVICE USED by more than 60% of all non-fiction authors, and so this approach to book-writing warrants a little time in the spotlight.

Gone are the days of ghostwriting being viewed as a shady, 'let's keep this under the radar' means to getting a book written well and sent out into the world. Now, professionals across the world—whether entrepreneurs and thought leaders, or celebrities and influencers— recognise the value of ghostwriting in articulately portraying their words, widening their net of impact, and sharing their mission with the huge bonuses and advantages that come with outsourcing:

Less time, greater professionalism, and the freedom to remain in your own zone of genius making money.

It's always been interesting to me that there has been so much resistance to hiring ghostwriters. As well-seasoned entrepreneurs and business owners, we, more so than non-business owners, tend to recognise and appreciate the value of doing only those things we do best and hiring professionals and experts to do the things we can't do to the standard to which we want it doing.

Dean Graziosi said this best: Smart entrepreneurs cut checks for speed. And I couldn't agree more, though my own addition to this would be that they cut checks for speed and quality.

There's no award for doing everything yourself—and, in certain circumstances, it really doesn't make sense to. Writing your own book might just be one of those circumstances. And it's in mind of this that I'm including this chapter—not only in this book full stop, but before you dive into outlining and blueprinting your book yourself—because you might just get to this point and reason that, yes, although you're sold on leveraging a book inside your business, the actual undertaking might just be better managed in someone else's more capable hands.

WHY YOU MIGHT OPT TO HIRE A GHOSTWRITER

There are various reasons why having your book ghostwritten might make a lot more sense than navigating the book-planning and -writing process yourself. Some pertain to time, while some relate to money—and others a combination. Others concern the overall quality of the book. I'll provide a general overview of these here.

TIME AND MONEY—THE BIG ONE

As a professional running a business or undertaking endeavours that can commonly mean high-ticket price points and large injections of cash coming into your business, when we consider the time needed to go through the entire process, it might make far more financial sense to opt for ghostwriting.

Let's consider the figures.

Let's say, for instance, that it tends to take you an average of ten hours to attract a lead, nurture that lead, and close them into a $10,000 service. That equates to you being able to earn $1,000 per hour when you are proactively and intentionally growing your business (in other words, not spending time in the service delivery/fulfilment stage or busying yourself with admin and general busyness). Of course, your services might require a much larger investment point and you might be able to move leads through the sales cycle far quicker, but just for the sake of ease and simplicity, we'll go with this.

Now let's imagine you're going to sit down and try to plan and write your book without any professional help (meaning no programs or courses, no mastermind, no coaching; nothing). When 'winging' the process, it can take an average of 150 hours to write a book. That's roughly three hours a week for a year (and that's not taking into account the time needed to research and source good editors, cover designers and a publisher).

If you were to instead direct those 150 hours to actively growing your business—very intentionally attracting in, nurturing, and closing leads—you could expect to generate $150,000 (assuming ten closes at $10,000 each across those 150 hours). This means that, if the cost of your ghostwriter falls below $150,000, you're in profit way before you even make money from your book.

Now, of course, ghostwriting rates vary, and this example provided here takes a medium-ticket price point with what I would argue is a lot of time spent actively nurturing (ten hours) for one close, so 150 hours might actually gross your business far more revenue. But even with this example, it's very evident that a turnkey ghostwriting solution—inclusive of book-planning, writing, and professional publication—would be a far better and more reasonable business, financial, and time investment.

One of my ghostwriting clients—who shall remain nameless, as all ghostwriting services are confidential—initially scheduled a call with me to discuss how I could guide her in writing her own book. When we talked through what that would look like—from both a time and investment standpoint—she asked me about ghostwriting. I explained how that might look for her, and the potential benefits and advantages. I then shared my Ghostwriting Calculator with her and guided her through the questions to establish whether ghostwriting might be a better fit. As soon as she saw the figures in combination with the time she would save, she opted for ghostwriting, signing the contract and paying immediately. Later, she told me it just made far more financial sense to take that route.

And it did.

(If you'd love to calculate more clearly whether ghostwriting would be a financial and time fit for your business, check out our free Ghostwriting Calculator; see the Resources page.)

TIME

Time, I would suggest, is the most precious resource we have in life—and although this can be seen in a number of different contexts every single day, it can be seen very clearly in the business context.

As above, when deciding to wing the journey that is planning and writing a book, it can prove to be quite costly (to the tune of 150 hours), and that's without considering the time you might also spend on trying to figure out and learn how to navigate the publication piece. (Note: Listening to friends about how you can self-publish on Amazon with a quick three-step process might be said with the purest of intentions, but it will ultimately cost you in ways far beyond time and money, but we'll discuss that in greater depth in Chapter 10.)

Although ghostwriting does still require some time, such as on video calls as your ghostwriter interviews you for content or recording voice clips to answer questions relating to content or reviewing content for approval, the time investment simply does not come even remotely close to the hundreds of hours you could spend doing it yourself.

One of my ghostwriting clients, who was talking through joining me in Mexico for the interview process, reasoned that she could couple working in a luxurious resort, making progress on her book (i.e. meeting with me to allow me to record her journey and gather material), while also holidaying (vacationing) and investing in self-care. Her investment into ghostwriting and publication, complete with the time spent working beachside on her business, presented a complete no-brainer of an avenue for writing and publishing a lead-generating book—and that's without the potential tax write-off for some businesses.

This same thread ran through a call I had with a very high-level entrepreneur in the 10X space, who wanted to hire me as his ghostwriter due to his time being far better spent in his business. For him, running workshops, guiding with his mentees, and appearing on huge stages across the world demanded his time more—but he still knew he needed a book to reach people not in his immediate orbit.

Essentially, as highlighted above, the time consideration comes down to where your time is best spent:

Is it best spent creating new intellectual property in your business, or writing your book?

Is it best spent vacationing or with your family, or writing your book?

Is it best spent nurturing and closing sales, or writing your book?

Is it best running global events, or writing your book?

As a general guiding point, my advice would be: if you prioritise spending your time in other areas but still see the huge value of leveraging a book in your business, ghostwriting is a worthwhile investment.

QUALITY

For me, this key factor is the absolute clincher and one of the most important reasons professionals hire a ghostwriter: quality.

In 2020, I was exchanging DMs with a prospective ghostwriting client (who again shall remain anonymous due to client confidentiality). She talked me through her life story—where she had started in life and where she had, at that time, progressed to be. As she discussed what she wanted to share in her book, she told me she had learned very early on in her professional life that there was an overarching, all-important need to be very intentional about the people she allowed into her sphere.

On that note, she went on to say that she made sure, in all areas of her life, that she was surrounded by those experts and professionals she knew could bring her vision to life faster and better than she could, because focusing on what you do best while bringing others in to 'pick up the slack'—specifically in those areas in which you don't excel or don't have expertise—is the recipe for success.

She hired me on the spot.

This sums up exactly why professionals across the world consider a ghostwriter before even considering writing a book themselves: because they have come to fully know, appreciate, and understand that it doesn't matter how good your book is when it's done; a professional will always be better positioned to take what would have been a *good* book and make it *great*.

Outsourcing the writing process is no different to outsourcing ads or marketing or video editing or any other of the many different tasks we entrepreneurs need to do—or get done—inside of our businesses. It makes sense to outsource any task that would be better produced with a professional onboard.

I CAN SPEAK, BUT I CAN'T WRITE

Over the past ten years, I've heard this statement countless times: *I can speak, but I can't write.* As someone far more inclined towards writing than doing lives, speaking onstage, or doing anything considered even remotely extroverted, it had never occurred to me when I first started in the industry that some people felt that they quite literally couldn't sit down to write a book—and that, if they did, it wouldn't come close to communicating the same value they do when they speak.

Fast-forward seventeen years in the publishing industry and ten years in our publishing house and I've come to learn that some people can see how valuable it would be to write and publish a book—predominantly in mind of securing more speaking opportunities—but they just can't stand the thought of actually tackling the project.

And that's quite literally how it feels; like it's an undertaking to be *tackled.*

This same sentiment was echoed by a ghostwriting client of mine very recently. Referred in by one of my incredible clients, she told me how she could talk and talk all day long, but she just couldn't sit down to write—hence why she needed me. For her, having someone more naturally aligned with writing was the absolute dream scenario: she would be able to tell her story while assigning the *workload* to a professional who would enjoy the entire process. Again, it proved to be a perfect match.

IN CONCLUSION

In conclusion, there are several different reasons people have for hiring a ghostwriter, and very few have anything to do with the author not being able to write or there being any component of laziness. In reality and in my own professional experience, the rationale for this choice tends to be strategic, business savvy, and financially justified.

Hiring a ghostwriter does not need to be viewed in any grubby light—and for me, it's the absolute opposite; it speaks into smart decision-making and weighing up any potential trade-off between time, money, and quality.

For some, writing their own book and being a part of that word-by-word process is part of the beauty and the magic of seeing their book come together. For others, however, there is something no less magical about simply talking with their ghostwriter and being sent first drafts of blueprints and excerpts and chapters flooding into their Inbox.

The book-writing process is beautiful and worthwhile—and that's the case ghostwriter or no ghostwriter.

ACTION STEPS: CHAPTER 14

1. Take a look at our Ghostwriting Calculator, fill in the fields, and identify for yourself whether, from a financial standpoint, a turnkey ghostwriting solution might be a better fit for you.
2. Encourage others in your circle to consider ghostwriting if they want to write a book but feel like any of the factors discussed in this chapter are reasons for them not yet taking action.
3. Share your thoughts, insights and key takeaways for Chapter 14 inside the Facebook group. How do you feel about ghostwriting after reading through this chapter?
www.facebook.com/groups/entrepreneurbooksuccess.

CHECKLIST: CHAPTER 14

1. Checked eligibility for ghostwriting.
2. Spread the word: ghostwriting isn't shady—it's a no-brainer!
3. Shared your thoughts, ideas and key takeaways about ghostwriting inside the Facebook group.

CHAPTER 15
FINAL WORDS

YOUR BOOK CAN BECOME SOMEONE'S FAVOURITE, IF ONLY
YOU HAVE THE COURAGE TO WRITE IT.

—HAYLEY PAIGE

International Bestselling Author, Entrepreneur and Ghostwriter

THE CLOSING CHAPTER; STRANGE BECAUSE, really, this is only the beginning.

It is my hope that, throughout the past two-hundred-plus pages, you have not only found a little help in moving forward, but a ton of golden nuggets that have not only positioned you to start and make progress, but inspired and excited you to such a point that you cannot wait to write and publish a book that can grow and enhance your business (or maybe even several).

What I have found throughout my career and the time spent dedicated to helping others to write their books and achieve new levels of success, whatever that may look like, is that starting is always the most difficult thing; deciding to go for it seems to always be the sticking point. But the beautiful thing here is that, by reading this book, you've already started. You've already shown a level of commitment to learning and progressing that so many others haven't shown.

What's incredibly interesting to me is that 86% of all Americans want to write a book, but only 3% of that 86% ever do. The dream falls by the wayside, and I know there's no genuine reason for that (time, money, skill); it's all fear-based.

To feel the fear and do it anyway is what the 1% do. I'm optimistic you, having read this book and maybe even having implemented some of the action steps detailed throughout, are in that 1%. I am—and I would love for you to join me.

So, as you embark on this journey, allow me to reiterate the important things:

The world needs your book.

You don't need to be a writer, you just need to be able to help your clients achieve results.

Your audience of Dream Clients need your book.

Your book isn't about you, it's about your readers.

To not write your book is to do a disservice to your audience.

Your book could become someone's favourite.

You bring something wonderful and unique in your combination of professional expertise, experience and *raw, real, and relatable*, and there's a hole in the world until your book is written and can fill it.

Not forgetting how incredibly powerful and lucrative a book can be in flooding your business with hot, ready-to-buy leads.

Because, of course:

Entrepreneur + Book = Success.

I thank you for reading this book, for seriously considering widening your net of impact, and for wanting to reach more people whom you can help. The next stage of this journey is set to be amazing. And I'd love to be there to help.

ACTION STEPS: CHAPTER 15

1. Get started!

CHECKLIST: CHAPTER 15

1. I started!

ACKNOWLEDGEMENTS

This book, like any and every project before it and those yet to come, is not the result of only my efforts; rather, this book has, in various ways, been written by a collective. Like raising a child and running a business, it's taken a village, even if all the villagers aren't fully aware of how they've contributed. This here is my opportunity to give a bit of a shoutout and send a sprinkling of love in the direction of each and every one of the villagers inside my community.

A special thank you to, in combination, Lisa and Rob: I will never forget the call that concluded with me telling you both I felt like I'd been bullied into putting my book out there! You both listened and heard me out, and validated my thoughts and feelings, before gently nudging me forward with a little bit of tough love. As the days became weeks, you both continued to tell me how much my people need this book. So, thank you for the reassurance, the pushes forward, and for giving me the time and space to see this through (even if that meant on-Zoom curries and chats instead of masterminds).

Faye: First, from a professional perspective, thank you for your advice and support across all stages of the journey, and for arranging your schedule in mind of prioritising this book. Your attention to detail and your evident want to make sure everything is exactly as it should be, not only for me and our publishing house, but for my readers and those who will soon become clients, are attributes I so appreciate in you. Every single day I am at once thankful for your role as our Chief Editor and in complete awe at your ability to manage a multitude of other clients and projects whilst maintaining standards that align with my potentially annoying perfectionism. Thank you.

And second, from a personal standpoint: Thank you for supporting this crazy dream of mine right from the get-go. It was 2013 and we'd been to hell and back, but you still encouraged me to do what my little girl self had always wanted to do. You poured support into me and helped me to achieve my dreams at every single point you could—despite being just nine years old! Would this publishing house be where it is now without you? I highly doubt it. And with that said, this book couldn't possibly have been written. So, my not-so-little first-born daughter, thank you for all the things. Together, we did it.

Amelia and Lane: You probably won't be able to appreciate until you're older how much the fun times spent between chapters have meant this book has come together so much more beautifully than if I hadn't had those moments with you. Thank you for the breaks spent on *Rainbow Friends* and *Among Us*. Thank you for the stickle bricks fights that had me howling in the kitchen. Thank you for being understanding of my need to cocoon myself away, either in the home office or inside our publishing house. And thank you for the endless cuddles (Lane) and continuous offers of espresso whilst checking that I'm eating (Amelia). I love you both so very much.

Uncle Graham: Thank you for gifting me the most special book of all, my very first hardcover, *The Adventures of The Secret Seven* by Enid Blyton, as published by Chancellor Press. That book was the all-important flap of a butterfly's wings, and it continues to be treasured.

Chrissy: My fellow entrepreneur, turned client, turned friend, turned bridesmaid, turned best friend. Your messages, love, support, kindness, sarcasm, wit, and no-bullshitness have kept me pursuing my dreams and goals, even when skies momentarily turned cloudy. You've kept me focused when other things have threatened to obscure my view, so thank you for that. Without you, I definitely would have missed some of my self-imposed deadlines for chapter completion—then where would I be?! Love you.

Michele Hayes: Probably completely unexpected, but you have been so pivotal in this journey—and probably without your realisation. It seems like any time I have wondered whether anyone will want to read this book, I've received a social media notification telling me you've tagged me in a recommendation or suggested someone reach out to me or declared how I'm the only publisher people should be considering! It seems like the universe has sent your words to me on so many different occasions throughout this period of writing, and it hasn't escaped my notice. Thank you for being the cheerleader and champion supporter you are. Your love has reached me half a world away.

Julie Stenberg: You have been such a shining light since I brought my publishing house into the entrepreneurial space in 2019 and embarked on my very first business mentorship. Not only have you shown complete loyalty and support throughout the past handful of years, but you've also been unknowingly influential in the direction my business has taken, especially when it came to crafting the *pièce de resistance*—the cherry on the sundae—in my publishing house. The words you spoke to me upon its creation have kept me moving forward, and they continue to inspire me every day. What you don't know is there are many other pieces when it comes to your influence and the story of our publishing house; these are best saved for another day. I do, however, promise to one day share those little tales with you. For now, let me say Thank You for all you have done, whether knowingly or not. The owl sitting on my shoulder will always carry with it a reminder.

And to the many different beautiful human beings whom I have come to know and love inside this entrepreneurial bubble; those who have never stopped encouraging me to do the next big thing and lending me their self-belief when I was low on my own:

Serena Hope Jones, Lorraine Schuchart, Scyller Borglum, Andee Hoig, Serena Skinner, Lauren Cope, Wendy Moore, Jessa Bellman, Ann Garner, Marie Kueny, Sharon Tasman, Phyllis Winters, Jamie Kim, Carrie Ryan, Shelley McLeod, Emma Grant, and the beautiful soul shining bright beyond this earth, Mary Swan-Bell.

And finally (but only because I'm saving the biggest Thank You till last), Rob (you deserve a mention that's all your own): Thank you for loving me. Thank you for knowing who I am, even when I haven't, and encouraging me to remember. Thank you for helping me to grow and thrive, even when I've had such moments of self-doubt that could have meant this book never being written. Thank you for the countryside drives and knowing how they recharge my soul so that I can get back to writing. Thank you for filling me up whenever you sensed I was getting close to empty. Thank you for helping me to continuously uplevel inside the business and therefore experience everything that has allowed me to bring this book to life. And thank you for keeping me in good food, good flowers, and good company throughout the journey. You know I love you so deeply there aren't the words. To me, you are everything.

RESOURCES

ONLINE PLATFORMS:

Websites:	www.onyxpublishing.com
	www.hayleypaigeinternational.com
LinkedIn:	www.linkedin.com/in/hayleypaigeinternational
Instagram:	www.instagram.com/hayleypaigeinternational
Facebook:	www.facebook.com/hayleypaigebookpublisher
Groups:	www.facebook.com/groups/
	femalecoachesandentrepreneurs
	www.facebook.com/groups/entrepreneurbooksuccess
Email:	hayley@entrepreneurbooksuccess.com

TOOLS AND ADDITIONAL TRAININGS:

Book Goals worksheet
www.entrepreneurbooksuccess.com/bookgoals

Mindset Mini Training
www.entrepreneurbooksuccess.com/mindset

Interviews with Clients
www.entrepreneurbooksuccess.com/interviews

Experience = Books Audit worksheet
www.entrepreneurbooksuccess.com/audit

Flip = Contents mini training
www.entrepreneurbooksuccess.com/flipcontents

FREE Million-Dollar Distribution Formula
www.entrepreneurbooksuccess.com/MDDF

How to Know When You're Done Checklist
www.entrepreneurbooksuccess.com/finish

Ghostwriting Calculator
www.onyxpublishing.com/ghostwritingcalculator

ADDITIONAL TOOLS

Tech, Automations and Systems Support for Your Business
www.facebook.com/groups/coaches.tech.automation

Free Demo (Automating Onboarding for Your Clients)
www.wowautomations.com/the-amazing-time-saving-automation-machine

NEXT STEPS

If you would love to further your journey with your lead-generating book, we have a number of options to help you, depending on the level of support you feel would be of benefit to you:

Our Blueprinting Program:
Self-guided; 12 months' access; Facebook group support.
www.onyxpublishing.co/non-fiction-success-blueprinting

2-Hour 1:1 Blueprinting Call:
High-touch 1:1.
www.onyxpublishing.co/121-blueprinting-mentoring

The Write and Publish Your Book Mastermind:
High-touch; 6-month group mastermind; with or without publication.
www.onyxpublishing.co/write-and-publish-your-book-mastermind

Our Publication Solution:
Comprehensive and professional; turnkey.
www.onyxpublishing.co

Hybrid Ghostwriting and Complete Ghostwriting:
High-touch, high-level service; comprehensive, completely turnkey.
www.onyxpublishing.com

***

And if you are intrigued and maybe even taken with the idea of launching your own publishing house, and if you love books and want to widen your net of impact, I would love to hear from you.

Successful Book Publishers: Complete Business Model™
(*Launch Your Own Publishing Company*):
Comprehensive; complete business solution; 6-figure investment.
www.hayleypaigeinternational.com/your-own-book-publisher

Milton Keynes UK
Ingram Content Group UK Ltd.
UKHW031533290724
446271UK00005B/351